WAY TO WISDOM

An Introduction to Philosophy

WAY TO WISDOM

An Introduction to Philosophy

by

KARL JASPERS

Translated by
RALPH MANHEIM

NEW HAVEN AND LONDON
YALE UNIVERSITY PRESS

Published in Great Britain, Europe, and Africa by
Yale University Press, Ltd., London.
Distributed in Latin America by Kaiman & Polon,
Inc., New York City; in Australasia by Book & Film
Services, Artarmon, N.S.W., Australia; in India by
UBS Publishers' Distributors Pvt. Ltd., Delhi;
in Japan by John Weatherhill, Inc., Tokyo.

CONTENTS

APPENDICES

I

WHAT IS PHILOSOPHY?

WHAT PHILOSOPHY IS and how much it is worth are matters of controversy. One may expect it to yield extraordinary revelations or one may view it with indifference as a thinking in the void. One may look upon it with awe as the meaningful endeavour of exceptional men or despise it as the superfluous broodings of dreamers. One may take the attitude that it is the concern of all men, and hence must be basically simple and intelligible, or one may think of it as hopelessly difficult. And indeed, what goes by the name of philosophy provides examples to warrant all these conflicting judgments.

For the scientific-minded, the worst aspect of philosophy is that it produces no universally valid results; it provides nothing that we can know and thus possess. Whereas the sciences in their fields have gained compellingly certain and universally recognized insights, philosophy, despite thousands of years of endeavour, has done nothing of the sort. This is undeniable: in philosophy there is no generally accepted, definitive knowledge. Any insight which for cogent reasons is recognized by all has ipso facto become scientific knowledge and ceased to be philosophy; its relevance is limited to a special sphere of the knowable.

Nor is philosophical thought, like the sciences, characterized by progressive development. Beyond any doubt, we are far more advanced than Hippocrates, the Greek physician. But we are scarcely entitled to say that we have progressed beyond Plato. We have only advanced beyond his materials, beyond the scientific findings of which he made use. In philosophy itself we have scarcely regained his level.

It lies in the very nature of philosophy, as distinguished from the sciences, that in any of its forms it must dispense with the unanimous recognition of all. The certainty to which it aspires is not of the objective, scientific sort, which is the same for every mind; it is an inner certainty in which a man's whole being participates. Whereas science always pertains to particular objects, the knowledge of which is by no means indispensable to all men, philosophy deals with the whole of being, which concerns man as man, with a truth which, wherever it is manifested, moves us more deeply than any scientific knowledge.

Systematic philosophy is indeed bound up with the sciences. It always reckons with the most advanced scientific findings of its time. But essentially philosophy springs from a different source. It emerges before any science, wherever men achieve awareness.

The existence of such a *philosophy without science* is revealed in several striking ways:

First: In philosophical matters almost everyone believes himself capable of judgment. Whereas it is recognized that in the sciences study, training, method are indispensable to understanding, in philosophy men generally assume that they are competent to form an opinion without preliminary study. Our own humanity, our own destiny, our own experience strike us as a sufficient basis for philosophical opinions.

This notion that philosophy must be accessible to all is justified. The circuitous paths travelled by specialists in philosophy have meaning only if they lead man to an awareness of being and of his place in it.

Second: Philosophical thought must always spring from free creation. Every man must accomplish it for himself.

A marvellous indication of man's innate disposition to philosophy is to be found in the questions asked by children. It is not uncommon to hear from the mouths of children words which penetrate to the very depths of philosophy. A few examples:

A child cries out in wonderment, "I keep trying to think that I am somebody else, but I'm always myself." This boy has touched on one of the universal sources of certainty, awareness of being through awareness of self. He is perplexed at the mystery of his I, this mystery that can be apprehended through nothing else. Questioningly, he stands before this ultimate reality.

Another boy hears the story of the Creation: In the beginning God made heaven and earth . . . and immediately asks, "What was before the beginning?" This child has sensed that there is no end to questioning, that there is no stopping place for the mind, that no conclusive answer is possible.

A little girl out walking in the woods with her father listens to his stories about the elves that dance in the clearings at night . . . "But there are no elves . . ." Her father shifts over to realities, describes the motion

9

of the sun, discusses the question of whether it is the sun or the earth that revolves, and explains the reasons for supposing that the earth is round and rotates on its axis . . . "Oh, that isn't so," says the little girl and stamps her foot. "The earth stands still. I only believe what I see." "Then," says her father, "you don't believe in God, you can't see Him either." The little girl is puzzled for a moment, but then says with great assurance, "If there weren't any God, we wouldn't be here at all." This child was seized with the wonder of existence: things do not exist through themselves. And she understood that there is a difference between questions bearing on particular objects in the world and those bearing on our existence as a whole.

Another little girl is climbing the stairs on her way to visit her aunt. She begins to reflect on how everything changes, flows, passes, as though it had never been. "But there must be something that always stays the same . . . I'm climbing these stairs on my way to see my aunt—that's something I'll never forget." Wonderment and terror at the universal transience of things here seek a forlorn evasion.

Anyone who chose to collect these stories might compile a rich store of children's philosophy. It is sometimes said that the children must have heard all this from their parents or someone else, but such an objection obviously does not apply to the child's really serious questions. To argue that these children do not continue to philosophize and that consequently such utterances must be accidental is to overlook the fact that children often possess gifts which they lose as they grow up. With the years we seem to enter into a prison of conventions and opinions, concealments and un-questioned acceptance, and there we lose the candour of childhood. The child still reacts spontaneously to the spontaneity of life; the child feels and sees and inquires into things which soon disappear from his vision. He forgets what for a moment was revealed to him and is surprised when grownups later tell him what he said and what questions he asked.

Third: Spontaneous philosophy is found not only in children but also in the insane. Sometimes—rarely—the veils of universal occlusion seem to part and penetrating truths are manifested. The beginning of certain mental disorders is often distinguished by shattering metaphysical revelations, though they are usually formulated in terms that cannot achieve significance: exceptions are such cases as Hölderlin and Van Gogh. But anyone witnessing these revelations cannot help feeling that the mists in which we ordinarily live our lives have been torn asunder. And many sane people have, in awaking from sleep, experienced strangely revealing insights which vanish with full wakefulness, leaving behind them only the impression that they can never be recaptured. There is profound meaning in the saying that children and fools tell the truth. But the creative originality to which we owe great philosophical ideas is not to be sought here but among those great minds—and in all history there have been only a few of them—who preserve their candour and independence.

Fourth: Since man cannot avoid philosophy, it is always present: in the proverbs handed down by tradition, in popular philosophical phrases, in dominant convictions such as are embodied in the idiom of the "emancipated," in political opinions, but most of all, since the very beginnings of history, in myths. There is no escape from philosophy. The question is only whether a philosophy is conscious or not, whether it is good or bad, muddled or clear. Anyone who rejects philosophy is himself unconsciously practising a philosophy.

What then is this philosophy, which manifests itself so universally and in such strange forms?

The Greek word for philosopher (*philosophos*) connotes a distinction from *sophos*. It signifies the lover of wisdom (knowledge) as distinguished from him who considers himself wise in the possession of knowledge. This meaning of the word still endures: the essence of philosophy is not the possession of truth but the search for truth, regardless of how many philosophers may belie it with their dogmatism, that is, with a body of didactic principles purporting to be definitive and complete. Philosophy means to be on the way. Its questions are more essential than its answers, and every answer becomes a new question.

But this on-the-wayness—man's destiny in time— contains within it the possibility of deep satisfaction, and indeed, in exalted moments, of perfection. This perfection never resides in formulable knowledge, in dogmas and articles of faith, but in a historical consummation of man's essence in which being itself is revealed. To apprehend this reality in man's actual situation is the aim of philosophical endeavour.

To be searchingly on the way, or to find peace and

the fulfilment of the moment—these are no definitions of philosophy. There is nothing above or beside philosophy. It cannot be derived from something else. Every philosophy defines itself by its realization. We can determine the nature of philosophy only by actually experiencing it. Philosophy then becomes the realization of the living idea and the reflection upon this idea, action and discourse on action in one. Only by thus experiencing philosophy for ourselves can we understand previously formulated philosophical thought.

But we can define the nature of philosophy in other ways. No formula can exhaust its meaning and none can be exclusive. In antiquity philosophy was defined (by its object) as the knowledge of things divine and human, the knowledge of being as being, or it was defined (by its aim) as learning how to die, as the striving for happiness by the exercise of thought; as an endeavour to resemble the divine; and finally (in the broadest sense) as the knowledge of all knowledge, the art of all arts, as *the* science—confined to no particular field.

Today perhaps we may speak of philosophy in the following terms; its aim is

to find reality in the primal source;

to apprehend reality in my thinking attitude toward myself, in my inner acts;

to open man to the Comprehensive in all its scope;

to attempt the communication of every aspect of truth from man to man, in loving contest;

patiently and unremittingly to sustain the vigilance

of reason in the presence of failure and in the presence of that which seems alien to it.

Philosophy is the principle of concentration through which man becomes himself, by partaking of reality.

Although philosophy, in the form of simple, stirring ideas, can move every man and even children, its conscious elaboration is never complete, must forever be undertaken anew and must at all times be approached as a living whole—it is manifested in the works of the great philosophers and echoed in the lesser philosophers. It is a task which man will face in one form or another as long as he remains man.

Today, and not for the first time, philosophy is radically attacked and totally rejected as superfluous or harmful. What is the good of it? It does not help us in affliction.

Authoritarian church thought has condemned independent philosophy on the ground that it is a worldly temptation which leads man away from God, destroys his soul with vain preoccupations. Political totalitarianism has attacked it on the ground that philosophers have merely interpreted the world in various ways, when the important thing was to change it. Both these schools of thought regarded philosophy as dangerous, for it undermined order, promoted a spirit of independence, hence of revolt, deluded man and distracted him from his practical tasks. Those who uphold another world illumined by a revealed God and those who stand for the exclusive power of a godless here and now would equally wish to extinguish philosophy.

And everyday common sense clamours for the simple yardstick of utility, measured by which philosophy again fails. Thales, who is regarded as the first of Greek philosophers, was ridiculed by a slave girl who saw him fall into a well while observing the sky. Why does he search the remote heavens when he is so awkward in his dealings with the things of this world?

Must philosophy then justify itself? That is impossible. It cannot justify itself on the basis of a something else for which it is useful. It can only appeal to the forces in every man which drive him toward philosophical thought. It is a disinterested pursuit, to which questions of utility or injuriousness have no relevance, an endeavour proper to man as man, and it will continue to fulfil this striving as long as there are men alive. Even those groups which are hostile to it cannot help harbouring their own peculiar ideas and bringing forth pragmatic systems which are a substitute for philosophy, though subservient to a desired end—such as Marxism or fascism. The existence of even these systems shows how indispensable philosophy is to man. Philosophy is always with us.

Philosophy cannot fight, it cannot prove its truth, but it can communicate itself. It offers no resistance where it is rejected, it does not triumph where it gains a hearing. It is a living expression of the basic universality of man, of the bond between all men.

Great systematic philosophies have existed for two and one-half millennia in the West, in China, and in India. A great tradition beckons to us. Despite the wide variety of philosophical thought, despite all the contradictions and mutually exclusive claims to truth, there is in all philosophy a One, which no man possesses but about which all serious efforts have at all times gravitated: the one eternal philosophy, the *philosophia perennis*. We must seek this historical foundation of our thinking if we would think clearly and meaningfully.

II

SOURCES OF PHILOSOPHY

THE HISTORY OF philosophy as methodical think-ing began twenty-five hundred years ago, but as mythical thought much earlier.

The beginning however is something quite different from the source. The beginning is historical and provides those who follow with a mounting accumula-tion of insights. But it is always from the source that the impulsion to philosophize springs. The source alone lends meaning to present philosophy and through it alone is past philosophy understood.

This source is of many kinds. Wonderment gives rise to question and insight; man's doubt in the know-ledge he has attained gives rise to critical examination and clear certainty; his awe and sense of forsakenness lead him to inquire into himself. And now let us examine these three drives.

First: Plato said that the source of philosophy was wonder. Our eyes gave us "the sight of the stars, the sun and the firmament." This "impelled us to examine the universe, whence grew philosophy, the greatest good conferred upon mortals by the gods." And Aristotle: "For it is owing to their wonder that men both now begin and at first began to philosophize: they wondered originally at the obvious difficulties, then advanced little by little and stated difficulties about the greater matters, e.g., about the phenomena of the moon, and those of the sun, and of the stars, and about the genesis of the universe."

Wonder impels man to seek knowledge. In my wonderment I become aware of my lack of knowledge. I seek knowledge, but for its own sake and not "to satisfy any common need."

In philosophical thought man awakens from his bondage to practical needs. Without ulterior purpose he contemplates things, the heavens, the world, and asks, what is all this? Where does it come from? From the answers to his questions he expects no profit but an intrinsic satisfaction.

Second: Once I have satisfied my wonderment and admiration by knowledge of what is, *doubt* arises. I have heaped up insights, but upon critical examination nothing is certain. Sensory perceptions are conditioned by our sense organs and hence deceptive; in any event they do not coincide with what exists in itself outside me, independently of my perception. Our categories are those of our human understanding. They become entangled in hopeless contradictions. Everywhere proposition stands against proposition. In my philosophical progress I seize upon doubt and attempt to apply it radically to everything, either taking pleasure in the sceptical negation which recognizes nothing but by itself cannot take a single step forward, or inquiring: Where then is there a certainty that rises above all doubt and withstands all critique?

Descartes' famous proposition, "I think, therefore I am," was for him a solid certainty, though he doubted everything else. For even a total fallacy in my thinking, a fallacy which may be beyond my under-standing, cannot blind me to the realization that in order to be deluded in my thinking I must *be*.

Methodical doubt gives rise to a critical examina-tion of all knowledge, and without radical doubt there can be no true philosophical thought. But the crucial question is: How and where has a foundation for certainty been gained through doubt itself?

And third: While I concentrate my energies upon the knowledge of things in the world, while I am engaged in doubt as a road to certainty, I am im-mersed in things; I do not think of myself, of my aims, my happiness, my salvation. In forgetfulness of my self I am content with the attainment of this know-ledge.

This changes when I become aware of myself in my situation.

The Stoic Epictetus said, "Philosophy arises when we become *aware of our own weakness and helplessness*." How shall I help myself in my weakness? His answer was: By looking upon everything that is not within my power as necessary and indifferent to me, but by raising what does depend on me, namely the mode and content of my ideas, to clarity and freedom by thought.

And now let us take a look at our human state. We are always in situations. Situations change, opportuni-ties arise. If they are missed they never return. I myself can work to change the situation. But there are situations which remain essentially the same even if their momentary aspect changes and their shattering

19

force is obscured: I must die, I must suffer, I must struggle, I am subject to chance, I involve myself inexorably in guilt. We call these fundamental situations of our existence ultimate situations.* That is to say, they are situations which we cannot evade or change. Along with wonder and doubt, awareness of these ultimate situations is the most profound source of philosophy. In our day-to-day lives we often evade them, by closing our eyes and living as if they did not exist. We forget that we must die, forget our guilt, and forget that we are at the mercy of chance. We face only concrete situations and master them to our profit, we react to them by planning and acting in the world, under the impulsion of our practical interests. But to ultimate situations we react either by obfuscation or, if we really apprehend them, by despair and rebirth: we become ourselves by a change in our consciousness of being.

Or we may define our human situation by saying that *no reliance can be placed in worldly existence*.

Ingenuously we mistake the world for being as such. In happy situations we rejoice at our strength, we are thoughtlessly confident, we know nothing but our actuality. In pain and weakness we despair. But if we come out of this situation alive we let ourselves slip back into forgetfulness of self and a life of happiness.

* The term here translated as "ultimate situation" is *Grenzsituation*. This is a concept of central importance for the understanding of Jaspers' thought, as for the understanding of Existentialism. As the context above shows, the ultimate situations are the inescapable realities in relation to which alone human life can be made genuinely meaningful. Ultimate situations cannot be changed or surmounted; they can only be acknowledged.

Such experience however has sharpened man's wits. The menace beneath which he lives drives him to seek security. He expects his mastery of nature and his community with other men to guarantee his existence.

Man gains power over nature in order to make it serve him; through science and technology he seeks to make it reliable.

But in man's domination of nature there remains an element of the incalculable which represents a constant threat, and the end is always failure: hard labour, old age, sickness and death cannot be done away with. Our dominated nature is reliable only in isolated cases; in the whole we can place no reliance.

Men band together in a community in order to limit and ultimately abolish the endless struggle of all against all; they seek to achieve security through mutual aid.

But here again there is a limit. Only if there were states in which every citizen stood to every other in a relation of absolute solidarity could justice and freedom be secure. For only then, if a citizen suffered injustice, would all others oppose it as one man. Such a state has never been seen. Those who have stood by one another in extremity and weakness have never been more than limited groups, and sometimes no more than a few individuals. No state, no church, no society offers absolute security. Such security has been a pleasing delusion of quiet times, in which the ultimate situations were veiled.

But there is a counterweight to the general

21

unreliability of the world: there are in the world things worthy of faith, things that arouse confidence; there is a foundation which sustains us: home and country, parents and ancestors, brothers and sisters and friends, husbands and wives. There is a foundation of historical tradition, in native language, in faith, in the work of thinkers, poets, and artists. However, this tradition also gives no security, it is not absolutely reliable. For we encounter it always as the work of man; God is nowhere in the world. Tradition always implies a question. Keeping sight of the tradition, man must always derive what for him is certainty, being, the reliable, from his own primal source. But the precariousness of all worldly existence is a warning to us, it forbids us to content ourselves with the world; it points to something else.

The ultimate situations—death, chance, guilt, and the uncertainty of the world—confront me with the reality of failure. What do I do in the face of this absolute failure, which if I am honest I cannot fail to recognize?

The advice of the Stoic, to withdraw to our own freedom in the independence of the mind, is not adequate. The Stoic's perception of man's weakness was not radical enough. He failed to see that the mind in itself is empty, dependent on what is put into it, and he failed to consider the possibility of madness. The Stoic leaves us without consolation; the independent mind is barren, lacking all content. He leaves us without hope, because his doctrine affords us no opportunity of inner transformation, no fulfilment through self-conquest in love, no hopeful expectation of the possible.

And yet the Stoics' striving is toward true philosophy. Their thought, because its source is in ultimate situations, expresses the basic drive to find a revelation of true being in human failure.

Crucial for man is his attitude toward failure: whether it remains hidden from him and overwhelms him only objectively at the end or whether he perceives it unobscured as the constant limit of his existence; whether he snatches at fantastic solutions and consolations or faces it honestly, in silence before the unfathomable. The way in which man approaches his failure determines what he will become.

In ultimate situations man either perceives nothingness or senses true being in spite of and above all ephemeral worldly existence. Even despair, by the very fact that it is possible in the world, points beyond the world.

Or, differently formulated, man seeks redemption. Redemption is offered by the great, universal religions of redemption. They are characterized by an objective guarantee of the truth and reality of redemption. Their road leads to an act of individual conversion. This philosophy cannot provide. And yet all philosophy is a transcending of the world, analogous to redemption.

To sum up: The source of philosophy is to be sought in wonder, in doubt, in a sense of forsakenness. In any case it begins with an inner upheaval, which determines its goal.

Plato and Aristotle were moved by wonder to seek the nature of being.

Amid infinite uncertainty Descartes sought compelling certainty.

Amid the sufferings of life the Stoics sought the repose of the mind.

Each of these experiences has its own truth, clothed always in historical conceptions and language. In making these philosophies our own we penetrate the historical husk to the primal sources that are alive within us.

The inner drive is toward firm foundations, depth of being, eternity.

But for us perhaps none of these is the most fundamental, absolute source. The discovery that being can be revealed to wonder is a source of inspiration, but beguiles us into withdrawing from the world and succumbing to a pure, magical metaphysic. Compelling certainty is limited to the scientific knowledge by which we orient ourselves in the world. Stoic imperturbability serves us only as a makeshift in distress, as a refuge from total ruin, but in itself remains without content and life.

These three motives—wonder leading to knowledge, doubt leading to certainty, forsakenness leading to the self—cannot by themselves account for our present philosophical thought.

In this crucial turning point in history, in this age of unprecedented ruin and of potentialities that can only be darkly surmised, the three motives we have thus far considered remain in force, but they are not adequate. They can operate only if there is *communication* among men.

In all past history there was a self-evident bond between man and man, in stable communities, in institutions, and in universal ideas. Even the isolated individual was in a sense sustained in his isolation. The most visible sign of today's disintegration is that more and more men do not understand one another, that they meet and scatter, that they are indifferent to one another, that there is no longer any reliable community or loyalty.

Today a universal situation that has always existed in fact assumes crucial importance: That I can, and cannot, become one with the Other in truth; that my faith, precisely when I am certain, clashes with other men's faith; that there is always somewhere a limit beyond which there appears to be nothing but battle without hope of unity, ending inevitably in subjugation or annihilation; that softness and complaisance cause men without faith either to band blindly together or stubbornly to attack one another.

All this is not incidental or unimportant. It might be, if there were a truth that might satisfy me in my isolation. I should not suffer so deeply from lack of communication or find such unique pleasure in authentic communication if I for myself, in absolute solitude, could be certain of the truth. But I am only in conjunction with the Other, alone I am nothing.

Communication from understanding to understanding, from mind to mind, and also from existence to existence, is only a medium for impersonal meanings and values. Defence and attack then become means not by which men gain power but by which they approach one another. The contest is a loving contest in which each man surrenders his weapons to the other. The certainty of authentic being resides only in unreserved communication between men who live together and vie with one another in a free community, who regard their association with one another as but a preliminary stage, who take nothing for granted and question everything. Only in communication is all other truth fulfilled, only in communication am I myself not merely living but fulfilling life. God manifests Himself only indirectly, and only through man's love of man; compelling certainty is particular and relative, subordinated to the Whole. The Stoical attitude is in fact empty and rigid.

The basic philosophical attitude of which I am speaking is rooted in distress at the absence of communication, in the drive to authentic communication, and in the possibility of the loving contest which profoundly unites self and self.

And this philosophical endeavour is at the same time rooted in the three philosophical experiences we have mentioned, which must all be considered in the light of their meaning, whether favourable or hostile, for communication from man to man.

And so we may say that wonder, doubt, the experience of ultimate situations, are indeed sources of philosophy, but the ultimate source is the will to authentic communication, which embraces all the rest. This becomes apparent at the very outset, for does not all philosophy strive for communication, express itself, demand a hearing? And is not its very essence communicability, which is in turn inseparable from truth?

Communication then is the aim of philosophy, and in communication all its other aims are ultimately rooted: awareness of being, illumination through love, attainment of peace.

Unity through truth
truth " unity

III

THE COMPREHENSIVE

HERE I SHOULD like to speak of one of the most difficult philosophical ideas. It is an indispensable idea, because it forms the foundation of all truly philosophical thinking. It must be intelligible in simple form, though its elaboration is a complex affair. I shall attempt to give an intimation of this idea.

Philosophy began with the question: What is? At first sight, there are many kinds of being, the things in the world, the forms of the animate and inanimate, all the infinitely many things that come and go. But what is true being, that is, the being which holds everything together, lies at the base of everything, the being from which everything that is issues?

To this there are curiously many answers. The first venerable answer of the first philosopher is: Everything is water and comes from water. Later thinkers said that everything is fundamentally fire or air or the indeterminate or matter, or atoms; or that life is primal being, from which inanimate things have merely degenerated; or that the mind is true being and that things are mere appearances, its ideas, which it produces as though in a dream. Thus we find a great number of metaphysical attitudes, which have been known as materialism (everything is matter and mechanical process), spiritualism (everything is spirit), hylozoism (the cosmos is a living spiritual

28

substance), and so on. In every case being was defined as something existing in the world, from which all other things sprang.

But which then is the correct view? Through thousands of years the warring schools have been unable to demonstrate the truth of any one of them. In each view some truth is manifested, namely an attitude and a method of inquiry which teach men to see something in the world. But each one becomes false when it lays claim to exclusiveness and strives to explain all existence.

Why is this so? All these views have one thing in common: they apprehend being as something which confronts me as an object, which stands apart from me as I think it. This basic phenomenon of our consciousness is to us so self-evident that we barely suspect the riddle it presents, because we do not inquire into it. The thing that we think, of which we speak, is always something other than ourselves, it is the object toward which we as subject are oriented. If we make ourselves into the object of our thinking, we ourselves become as it were the Other, and yet at the same time we remain a thinking I, which thinks about itself but cannot aptly be thought as an object because it determines the objectness of all objects. We call this basic condition of our thinking the subject-object dichotomy. As long as we are awake and conscious we are always involved in it. Twist and turn as we will we are always in this dichotomy, always oriented toward an object, whether the object be the reality of our sense perception, whether it be the concept of ideal objects, such as numbers or geometrical figures, or whether it be a fantasy or even an impossible imagining. We are always confronted outwardly or inwardly by objects, which are the content of our consciousness. As Schopenhauer said, there is no object without a subject and no subject without an object.

What is the meaning of this ever-present subject-object dichotomy? It can only mean that being as a whole is neither subject nor object but must be the Comprehensive, which is manifested in this dichotomy.

Being :

Clearly being as such cannot be an object. Everything that becomes an object for me breaks away from the Comprehensive in confronting me, while I break away from it as subject. For the I, the object is a determinate being. The Comprehensive remains obscure to my consciousness. It becomes clear only through objects, and takes on greater clarity as the objects become more conscious and more clear. The Comprehensive does not itself become an object but is manifested in the dichotomy of I and object. It remains itself a background, it boundlessly illumines the phenomenon, but it is always the Comprehensive.

But there is in all thinking a second dichotomy. Every determinate object is thought in reference to other objects. Determinacy implies differentiation of the one from the other. And even when I think of being as such, I have in mind nothingness as its antithesis.

Thus every object, every thought content stands in a twofold dichotomy, first in reference to me, the thinking subject, and secondly in reference to other objects. As thought content it can never be everything, never the whole of being, never being itself. Whatever is thought must break out of the Comprehensive. It is a particular, juxtaposed both to the I and to other objects.

Thus in our thinking we gain only an intimation of the Comprehensive. It is not manifested to us, but everything else is manifested in it.

What are the implications of this idea?

Measured by our customary understanding in relation to things, it seems unnatural. Our understanding, attuned to the practical, resists it.

The basic operation by which we raise ourselves above everything that is thought is perhaps not difficult, but it seems strange because it does not bring knowledge of a new object which we then apprehend, but aspires with the help of the idea to transform our consciousness of being.

Because it shows us no new object, the idea, measured by our customary worldly knowledge, is empty. But by its form it opens up to us infinite possibilities in which being may manifest itself to us, and at the same time lends transparency to everything that is. It transforms the meaning of the world of objects, by awakening in us a faculty of sensing what authentically *is* in the phenomenon.

Let us attempt a further step toward the elucidation of the Comprehensive.

To philosophize concerning the Comprehensive

would mean to penetrate into being itself. This can only be done indirectly. For even as we speak we are engaged in object thinking. Through object thinking we must gain indices to the nonobject, that is to the Comprehensive.

An example is the thought operation we have just performed. The moment we state the subject-object dichotomy in which we always find ourselves and which we cannot see from outside, we make it into an object. But this is basically incongruous. For dichotomy is a relation between things in the world which confront me as objects. This relation becomes an image by which to express what is not visible and can itself never become object.

Still thinking in images, we ascertain through the source that is present within us a polyvalence in this subject-object dichotomy. It is fundamentally different, depending on whether I as understanding am oriented toward objects; as *Dasein*, being-there, toward my environment; or as existence toward God.

As understanding we confront tangible things, and to a certain measure we succeed in obtaining compelling and universally valid knowledge, but always of determinate objects.

As being-there, as men living in our environment, we experience in it what we perceive with our senses, what achieves reality for us as the presence which cannot be reduced to universal knowledge.

As existence we are oriented toward God—transcendence—and this through the language of things, which existence uses as hieroglyphics or symbols. Neither our understanding nor our vital sensualism apprehends the reality of this symbolism. God as object is a reality only for us as existence; He is situated in an entirely different dimension from the empirical, sensible objects susceptible to compelling knowledge.

Thus the Comprehensive, when we seek to apprehend it, breaks down into several modes; according to the three modes of the subject-object dichotomy, we have seen it break down into (1) the understanding, *universal thought* or consciousness as such, as which we are all identical; (2) being-there, as which we are each of us a particular *particular* individual; (3) existence, as which we are authentically ourselves in our historicity.

I cannot elaborate on this statement in this brief space. Suffice it to say that the Comprehensive, conceived as being itself, is called transcendence (God) and the world, while as that which we ourselves are it is called being-there, consciousness, mind, and existence.

Now that, with our basic philosophical operation, we have loosened the fetters binding us to objects mistaken for being itself, we are in a position to understand the meaning of *mysticism*. For thousands of years philosophers in China, India, and the West have given utterance to a thought which is everywhere and at all times the same, though diverse in its expression: man can transcend the subject-object dichotomy and achieve a total union of subject and object, in which all objectness vanishes and the I is extinguished. Then authentic being opens up to us, leaving behind it as we awaken from our trance a consciousness of profound and inexhaustible meaning. For him who has experienced it, this becoming one is the true awakening, and the awakening to consciousness in the subject-object dichotomy is more in the nature of sleep. Plotinus, the greatest mystical philosopher of the West, writes:

"Often when I awaken to myself from the slumber of the body, I behold a wondrous beauty: I then believe firmly that I belong to a better and higher world, I call forth the most glorious life within me, I have become one with the godhead."

We cannot doubt the existence of mystical experience, nor can we doubt that mystics have always been unable to communicate what is most essential in their experience. The mystic is immersed in the Comprehensive. The communicable partakes of the subject-object dichotomy, and a clear consciousness seeking to penetrate the infinite can never attain the fullness of that source. We can speak only of that which takes on object form. All else is incommunicable. But its presence in the background of those philosophical ideas which we call speculative constitutes their content and meaning.

On the basis of our philosophical inquiry into the Comprehensive, we shall be better able to understand the great metaphysical theories of history, the theories of fire, matter, the mind, the world process, etc. For in reality they were not solely the object knowledge as which they are often interpreted, and considered as which they are completely false; they were hieroglyphics of being, devised by the philosophers out of the presence of the Comprehensive, for the elucidation of the self and of being—and then at once mistaken for positive objectivizations of authentic being.

When we move amid the phenomena of the world, we come to realize that we possess being itself neither in the object, which becomes continuously more restricted, nor in the horizon of our always limited world taken as the sum of phenomena, but only in the Comprehensive which transcends all objects and horizons, which transcends the subject-object dichotomy.

Once we have ascertained the Comprehensive through our basic philosophical operation, we realize that all the metaphysics we have listed, all those supposed insights into being, are in error as soon as they interpret anything that is in the world, however important and significant, as being itself. But they are the only language in which we can speak when we transcend all objects, ideas, world horizons, phenomena, to perceive being itself.

For we do not attain this goal by leaving the world, except in incommunicable mysticism. Only in articulate object knowledge can our consciousness remain clear. Only in object knowledge, experiencing its limits through what it surmises at the limit, can our consciousness achieve content. Even in the thinking which transcends object knowledge we remain in it. Even when we see through the phenomenon it holds us fast.

Through metaphysics we obtain an intimation of the Comprehensive in transcendence. We understand this metaphysics as a symbol.

But we lose its meaning if we succumb to irresponsible aesthetic enjoyment of its ideas. For its content is manifested to us only if we perceive the reality in the symbol. And we perceive it only out of the reality of our existence and not out of mere understanding, which in this sphere declines to see any meaning at all.

But above all we must not look on the symbol of reality as a physical reality like the things which we grasp, live with, and consume. To regard the object as being is the essence of all dogmatism, and to mistake the materiality of symbols for reality is specifically the essence of superstition. For superstition is chained to the object, faith is rooted in the Comprehensive.

And now the last methodological consequence of our experience of the Comprehensive: the consciousness of the discontinuity of our philosophical thinking.

When we think of the Comprehensive in philosophical terms, we are making an object of what is essentially not an object. Hence we must always make a reservation: we must retract the object content of what has been said, if we would arrive at that experience of the Comprehensive which is not a communicable content resulting from inquiry but an attitude of our consciousness. It is not my knowledge but my consciousness of being that changes.

But this is a basic trait of all true philosophical thought. Man soars to the Comprehensive in the medium of determinate object thinking, and only in that medium. He actualizes in consciousness the foundation of our life in being, the guidance from that sphere, the basic mood and meaning of our life and activity; he frees us from the fetters of determinate thinking, not by relinquishing it but by carrying it to the extreme. In the general philosophical idea he leaves room for its realization in the present.

Being can only be for us on condition that it become present to the mind in the dichotomy of subject and object. Hence our drive toward clarity. That which is present only obscurely must be apprehended in object form, out of the essence of the I fulfilling itself. Being itself, the foundation of all things, the absolute, presses upon our consciousness in object form which, because as object it is inadequate, disintegrates, leaving behind the pure clarity of the presence of the Comprehensive.

Awareness of the subject-object dichotomy as the fundamental fact of our thinking existence and of the Comprehensive that becomes present in it gives us the freedom needed for philosophy.

It is an idea that frees us from every existent. It compels us to turn back from the impasse of absolutization. It is as it were an idea that turns us about.

For those who found support in the absoluteness of things and in a theory of knowledge confined to objects, the loss of them is nihilism. Exclusive reality and truth cannot be imputed to that which discourse and object thinking have made determinate and hence finite.

Our philosophical thinking passes through this nihilism, which is in truth a liberation for authentic being. By our rebirth in philosophy the meaning and value of all finite things, though always limited, are enhanced; we are made fully aware that our roads must lead through them, but at the same time we achieve the only possible basis for freedom in our dealings with these things.

The fall from absolutes which were after all illusory becomes an ability to soar; what seemed an abyss becomes space for freedom; apparent Nothingness is transformed into that from which authentic being speaks to us.

IV

THE IDEA OF GOD

Our western idea of God springs from two historical roots: the Bible and Greek philosophy.

When Jeremiah saw the ruin of everything for which he had worked all his life, when his country and his people were lost, when in Egypt the last remnants of his people turned aside from their faith in Yahweh and offered sacrifices to Isis, and when his disciple Baruch despaired, "I fainted in my sighing, and I find no rest," Jeremiah answered, "Behold, that which I have built will I break down, and that which I have planted I will pluck up, even this whole land. And seekest thou great things for thyself? seek them not."

In such a situation these words mean: It is enough that God is. Do not ask whether there is immortality; the question of whether God forgives is no longer important. Man no longer matters, his defiance as well as his concern for his own beatitude and eternity is extinguished. It is also impossible that the world should have a purpose susceptible of fulfilment, that it should endure in any form; for everything has been created out of nothing by God and is in His hand. When everything is lost, but one thing remains: God is. If a life in this world, even with faith in God's guidance, has failed, this overpowering reality still remains: God is. If man fully renounces himself and his aims, this reality can be manifested to him as the only reality. But it does not manifest itself in advance, it does not manifest itself abstractly, but descends into the existence of the world, and only here manifests itself at the limit. Jeremiah's words are hard words. They are no longer bound up with any will to historical efficacy in the world, though such a will has preceded them throughout a lifetime and ultimately, through total failure, made them possible. They are simple words, free from imaginative flight, and they contain unfathomable truth, precisely because they are without finite content or any fixation in the world.

The Greek philosophers expressed a similar thought in different terms.

At about 500 B.C. Xenophanes proclaimed: There is only one God, resembling mortals neither in his aspect nor in his thoughts. Plato conceived of the godhead—he called it the Good—as the source of all knowledge. Not only is the knowable known in the light of the godhead; it also derives its being from the godhead which excels being both in rank and power.

The Greek philosophers understood that the many gods were decreed merely by custom, whereas in nature there was only one God; that God is not seen with our eyes, that he resembles no one and can be recognized in no image.

God is conceived as cosmic reason or cosmic law, or as fate and providence, or as demiurge.

But this God of the Greek thinkers is a God originating in thought, not the living God of Jeremiah. In essence the two coincide. From this twofold root

40

Western theology and philosophy have, in infinite modulations, reflected that God is and pondered on what He is.

The philosophers of our day seem to evade the question of whether God exists. They do not say that He exists nor do they deny His existence. But anyone engaging in philosophical thought must answer for his opinions. If a philosopher doubts, he must say why, else he cannot progress beyond the sceptical philosophy which asserts nothing at all, which affirms nothing and denies nothing. Or, limiting himself to determinate object knowledge, that is to scientific cognition, he ceases to philosophize, saying: It is best not to talk of what we do not know.

The question of God is discussed on the basis of conflicting propositions which we shall examine.

The theological proposition is: We can know of God only because He revealed Himself to certain men from the prophets to Jesus. Without revelation God can have no reality for man. God is accessible not through thought but through faith and obedience.

But long before and far outside the world of biblical revelation there was certainty as to the reality of the godhead. And within the world of the Christian West many men have derived certainty of God without the guarantee of revelation.

There is an old philosophical proposition opposed to this theological doctrine: We know of God because His existence can be proved. The proofs for the existence of God form an impressive document.

41

But if the proofs for the existence of God are construed as scientifically compelling proofs such as we find in mathematics or the empirical sciences, they are false. In this light Kant radically confuted them.

Then came the reverse proposition: Since all proofs of the existence of God can be refuted, there is no God.

This inference is false. For the nonexistence of God can be proved no more than his existence. The proofs and their confutations show us only that a proved God would be no God but merely a thing in the world.

The truth, as against all supposed proofs and refutations of the existence of God, seems to be this: The so-called proofs of the existence of God are fundamentally no proofs at all, but methods of achieving certainty through thought. All the proofs of the existence of God and their variants that have been devised through the centuries differ essentially from scientific proofs. They are attempts to express the experience of man's ascent to God in terms of thought. There are roads of thought by which we come to limits at which the consciousness of God suddenly becomes a natural presence.

Let us consider a few examples:

The oldest of proofs is the cosmological proof. From the existence of the cosmos (the Greek name for universe) we infer that God exists; from the world process, in which everything is effect, we infer a last cause; from motion the source of all motion; from the accident of the particular the necessity of the whole.

If by this syllogism we mean to infer the existence of one thing from the existence of another thing, as we do for example in inferring from the existence of the side of the moon which faces us the existence of the other side which we never see, it is inapplicable. In this manner we can only infer the existence of things in the world from the existence of other things. The world as a whole is not an object, because we are always in it and we never confront the world as a whole. Hence we cannot, from the existence of the world as a whole, infer the existence of something other than the world.

But this notion takes on a new meaning when it is no longer regarded as a proof. Then metaphorically, in the form of an inference, it expresses awareness of the mystery inherent in the existence of the world and of ourselves in it. If we venture the thought that there might be nothing, and ask with Schelling: Why is there something and not nothing? we find that our certainty of existence is such that though we cannot determine the reason for it we are led by it to the Comprehensive, which by this very essence is and cannot not be, and through which everything else is.

True, men have looked on the world as eternal and said that it existed out of itself and hence was identical with God. But this is not possible:

Everything in the world which is beautiful, appropriate, ordered, and embodies a certain perfection—the vast abundance of things that fill us with emotion in our immediate contemplation of nature—all this cannot be apprehended through any fully knowable worldly thing, through matter, for example. The design of organic life, the beauty of nature in all its forms, the order of the universe in general become increasingly mysterious as our knowledge advances.

But if from all this we infer that God, the benevolent creator, exists, we must call to mind all that is ugly, disordered, base in the world. And this gives rise to fundamental attitudes for which the world is alien, frightening, terrible, and it seems as plausible to infer the existence of the devil as of God. The mystery of transcendence is not thereby solved but merely grows deeper.

But what clinches the matter is the imperfectibility of the world. The world is not finished, but in continuous change; our knowledge of the world cannot be completed, the world cannot be apprehended through itself.

Far from proving the existence of God, these so-called proofs mislead us into placing God within the real world, or second cosmos, which is as it were ascertained at the limits of the cosmos. Thus they obscure the idea of God.

But they move us deeply when, leading through the concrete phenomena of the cosmos, they confront Nothingness and imperfectibility. For then they seem to admonish us not to content ourselves with the world as the sole meaning of our life in the world.

Again and again it is brought home to us that God is not an object of knowledge, of compelling evidence. He cannot be experienced by the senses. He is invisible, He cannot be seen but only believed in.

But whence comes this faith? Its source is not in the limits of worldly experience but in the freedom of man.

The man who attains true awareness of his freedom gains certainty of God. Freedom and God are inseparable. Why?

This I know: in my freedom I am not through myself, but am given to myself, for I can fail myself and I cannot force my freedom. Where I am authentically myself, I am certain that I am not through myself. The highest freedom is experienced in freedom from the world, and this freedom is a profound bond with transcendence.

We also call man's freedom his existence. My certainty of God has the force of my existence. I can have certainty of Him not as a content of science but as presence for existence.

If certainty of freedom encompasses certainty of God's existence, there must be a connection between the negation of freedom and the negation of God. If I do not experience the miracle of selfhood, I need no relation to God, I am content with the empirical existence of nature, many gods, demons.

There is, on the other hand, a connection between the belief that there can be freedom without God and the deification of man. This is an illusory, arbitrary freedom, in which man's will is taken to be absolute and independent. I rely in the force of my will and in a defiant acceptance of death. But this delusion that I am through myself alone turns freedom into perplexity and emptiness. A savage drive for self-assertion turns to a despair, in which Kierkegaard's "desperate will to be oneself" and "desperate will not to be oneself" become one.

God exists for me in the degree to which I in freedom

45

authentically become myself. He does not exist as a scientific content but only as openness to existence.

But the illumination of our existence as freedom does not prove the existence of God; it merely points, one might say, to the area in which certainty of his existence is possible.

The thought that strives for compelling certainty cannot realize its aim in any proof of God's existence. But the failure of thought does not result in nothingness. It points to that which resolves into an inexhaustible, forever-questioning, Comprehensive consciousness of God.

God never becomes a tangible object in the world—and this means that man must not abandon his freedom to the tangibilities, authorities, powers of the world; that he bears responsibility for himself, and must not evade this responsibility by renouncing freedom ostensibly for the sake of freedom. He must owe his decision and the road he chooses to himself. Kant has said that God's unfathomable wisdom is as admirable in what it gives us as in what it denies us. For if God's wisdom in its majesty were always before our eyes, if it were an absolute authority, speaking unequivocally in the world, we should be puppets of its will. But God in his wisdom wanted us to be free.

Instead of the knowledge of God, which is unattainable, we gain through philosophy a Comprehensive consciousness of God.

"God is." The essential in this proposition is the

reality to which it points. We do not encompass this reality in thinking the proposition; merely to think it leaves us empty. For it means nothing to the understanding and to sensory experience. We apprehend its meaning only as we transcend, as we pass beyond the world of objects and through it discover authentic reality. Hence the climax and goal of our life is the point at which we ascertain authentic reality, that is, God.

This reality is accessible to existence through the orientation toward God that lies at its source. Hence faith in God, springing as it does from the source, resists any mediation. This faith is not laid down in any definite articles of faith applicable to all men or in any historical reality which mediates between man and God and is the same for all men. The individual, always in his own historicity, stands rather in an immediate, independent relation to God that requires no intermediary.

This historicity, which can be communicated and described, is in this form not absolute truth for all, and yet in its source it is absolutely true.

God is reality, absolute, and cannot be encompassed by any of the historical manifestations through which He speaks to men. If He is, man as an individual must be able to apprehend Him directly.

The reality of God and the immediacy of our historical relation to God exclude any universally compelling knowledge of God; therefore what matters is not our knowledge of God but our attitude towards God. From time immemorial God has been conceived in empirical forms, including a personification after the image of man. And yet every such conception is at the same time in the nature of a veil. God is not what we may see with our eyes.

Our true attitude toward God has found its profoundest expression in a few biblical injunctions:

Thou shalt not make unto thee any graven image or likeness. This meant, to begin with, that because God is invisible man must not worship Him in statues, idols, effigies. Gaining in depth, this tangible prohibition developed into the idea that God is not only invisible but also inconceivable, unthinkable. No symbol or metaphor can describe Him and none may take His place. All metaphorical representations of God without exception are myths, meaningful as such when understood to be mere hints and parallels, but they become superstitions when mistaken for the reality of God Himself.

Since every image conceals as much as it discloses, we come closest to God in the negation of images. But even in the Bible this Old Testament commandment was not fulfilled: the image of God's personality remained—His wrath and His love, His justice and His mercy. It is a commandment that cannot be fulfilled. Parmenides and Plato, with their speculative doctrines of being, the Indian Brahman philosophers, the Chinese Taoists attempted to apprehend without images the suprapersonal, pure, intangible reality of God—but in this they did not succeed. Human thought and human vision cannot dispense with the image. And though in philosophical thinking sensation and object almost vanished, perhaps ultimately some wisp of God's presence remains, with power to engender life.

Then, even after philosophy has rationally elucidated the deification of nature, the purely demonic, the aesthetic and superstitious, the specifically numinous, the deepest mystery is still not expelled.

Perhaps we can give some paraphrase of this presence of God at the end of philosophical endeavour.

It is the silence in the face of being. Speech ceases in the presence of that which is lost to us when it becomes object.

This ultimate can be attained only in the transcending of all thought. It cannot itself be transcended. Before it lies contentment with one's lot and the extinction of all desire.

Here is a haven and yet no fixed home. Here is a repose that can sustain us amid the inevitable unrest of our wanderings in the world.

Here thought must dissolve into radiance. Where there is no further question, there is also no answer. In the philosophical transcending of question and answer we arrive at the limit, at the stillness of being.

Another biblical injunction runs: *Thou shalt have no other gods before me.* At first this commandment implied a rejection of alien gods. Gaining in depth, it became a simple and unfathomable idea: there is only one God. The life of the man who believes in the one and only God rests on a foundation entirely different from that of a life with many gods. Concentration on the One gives to the decision of existence its real foundation. Infinite wealth implies diffusion; God's glory is not absolute unless it is grounded in the One. The quest for the One as the foundation of his life is an

49

enduring problem for man, as actual as it was thousands of years ago.

A third biblical saying: *Thy will be done*. This fundamental attitude toward God means: Bow down before that which defies understanding, confident that it is situated above and not below the understandable. "Thy thoughts are not our thoughts, thy ways are not our ways."

Trust in this basic attitude makes possible an all-encompassing sense of thankfulness, a wordless, impersonal love.

Man stands before the godhead as the hidden God and can accept what is most terrible as His decision, fully aware that in whatever finite form he expresses this God it is spoken in human terms and hence false.

To sum up: Our attitude toward the godhead is defined by the commandments "No image and no likeness," "No other god," and by the attitude of acceptance expressed in the words "Thy will be done."

Reflection on God clarifies our faith. But to believe is not to see. God remains in the distance and remains question. To live by God does not mean to base oneself on calculable knowledge but to live as though we staked our existence on the assumption that God is.

To believe in God means to live by something which is not in the world, except in the polyvalent language of phenomena, which we call the hieroglyphs or symbols of transcendence.

The God of faith is the distant God, the hidden God, the indemonstrable God.

Hence I must recognize not only that I do not know

God but even that I do not know whether I believe. Faith is no possession. It confers no secure knowledge, but it gives certainty in the practice of life.

Thus the believer lives in the enduring ambiguity of the objective, in enduring willingness to hear. He listens patiently and yet he is unswerving in his resolve. In the cloak of weakness he is strong, he is open, though in his real life he is resolute.

Reflection on God is typical of all significant philosophical thought: it does not bring secure knowledge, but to authentic self-hood it gives a free area for decision; the whole emphasis is on love in the world, on the reading of the symbols of transcendence, on the depth and breadth of that which is illumined by reason.

That is why all philosophical discourse is so incomplete. It calls for completion out of the being of him who hears it.

Philosophy does not give, it can only awaken—it can remind, and help to secure and preserve.

In it each of us understands what he actually knew before.

V

THE UNCONDITIONAL IMPERATIVE

In LOVE, IN battle, in pursuing lofty tasks, men often act without regard for consequences, unconditionally. When a man acts unconditionally his life is not the ultimate, he subordinates it to something else.

When we obey the unconditional imperative, our empirical existence becomes in a sense the raw material of the idea, of love, of a loyalty. It is encompassed in an eternal aim, it is as it were consumed, and it is not allowed drift at random in the stream of life. Only at the limit, in extreme situations, can the call of the unconditional lead to loss of life, to acceptance of inevitable death, while in bondage to the conditional we wish first, last, and at any price to preserve our physical existence.

Men have, for example, risked their lives in a common struggle for a common life in the world. Solidarity was then the ultimate condition.

Originally such communities were built upon trust but later they came to be based on the inspiring command of an authority in which men believed, so that faith in this authority became a source of the absolute. This faith freed men from uncertainty, spared them the need to inquire for themselves. However, the unconditional in this form was subject to a tacit condition, namely the success of the authority. The believer desired to live through his obedience. If the authority ceased to be successful as a power, and men lost their faith in it, a ruinous emptiness arose.

And the only escape from this emptiness is for man himself as an individual to win authentic being as the foundation of his decisions.

This has happened in history when individuals staked their lives through obedience to an absolute imperative: they remained loyal where disloyalty would have destroyed everything, where a life saved through disloyalty would have been poisoned, where a betrayal of absolute being would have made a saved life wretched.

The purest example is perhaps Socrates. Living in the lucidity of his reason, out of the Comprehensive of nonknowledge, he went his way unswervingly, undeterred by the passions of anger, hatred, selfrighteousness; he made no concession, refused to avail himself of the opportunity for flight, and died happy, staking everything on his faith.

Certain martyrs, like Thomas More, have displayed the purest moral energy in their faith. The martyrdom of some others is subject to question. To die for something in order to bear witness to it is to give an aim to one's death, hence to make it impure. Where martyrs have actually been inspired by a longing to die, perhaps in imitation of Christ, by a death urge which not infrequently darkens the soul with symptoms of hysteria, the impurity is still greater.

Rare are the philosophers who, without firm allegiance to a community of faith, standing alone before God, have realized the maxim: To philosophize is to learn how to die. Seneca, for years awaiting his death sentence, overcame the desire to escape dictated by his understanding; in the end he did not betray himself by unworthy actions, and he preserved his composure when Nero demanded his death. Boethius died innocently, sentenced by a barbarian: he died philosophizing in full lucidity, turned toward authentic being. Bruno overcame his doubts and withdrew what concessions he had made, in the high resolve to stand fast for no purpose, even if it meant death at the stake.

Seneca, Boethius, Bruno were men with their weaknesses, their failures, men such as ourselves. They had to conquer themselves. And this is why they can point the way for us. For saints after all are figures who for us can live only in the twilight, or in the unreal light of myth, but cannot stand up under realistic scrutiny. The unconditional acts of which men as men were capable give us true encouragement, while the imaginary provides only empty edification.

We have recalled historical examples of men who know how to die. Let us now attempt to elucidate the unconditional imperative.

When I ask myself: What shall I do? I arrive at an answer by adducing finite aims and means by which to attain them. I must obtain food and for this work is needed. I must live with men in a community: here I am helped by certain rules of conduct. In every case an aim determines the means appropriate to it.

But my basis for recognizing these aims lies either in some unquestioned practical interest or in utility. Empirical existence, however, is no ultimate end, because the questions remain: What kind of existence? and What for?

Or else the imperative is grounded in an authority which I must obey because someone else has willed it or because "It is written." But such authority remains unquestioned and hence unexamined.

All such imperatives are conditional. For they make me dependent on something outside me, on practical aims or authority. Unconditional imperatives on the other hand have their source in myself. Conditional imperatives confront me as fixed but transient principles, by which I can outwardly sustain myself. Unconditional imperatives come from within me, sustaining me inwardly by that which in myself is not only myself.

The unconditional imperative comes to me as the command of my authentic self to my mere empirical existence. I become aware of myself as of that which I myself am, because it is what I ought to be. This awareness is obscure at the beginning and lucid at the end of my unconditional action. When we become aware of the imperative our questioning ceases in the certainty of being—though in temporal life there is at once a new beginning of questioning, and in a changed situation certainty must forever be gained anew.

This imperative precedes every aim, it is that which determines all aims. Accordingly it is not an object of our will but its source.

The unconditional is a foundation of action and hence not an object of knowledge but an element of faith. In so far as I know the reasons and aims of my action, I am in the finite, I am subject to conditions.

Only when I live by something that can no longer be explained by object knowledge do I live by the unconditional.

A few propositions may suggest the meaning of the unconditional imperative.

First: as opposed to passive acceptance of things as they are, the unconditional attitude implies a decision, lucidly taken, out of an unfathomable depth, a decision with which I myself am identical. What does this mean?

It means to partake in the eternal, in being. Accordingly, it implies absolute reliability and loyalty, which derive not from nature but from our decision. The decision is arrived at only through lucidity which is the product of reflection. Expressed in psychological terms, the unconditional attitude does not lie in the momentary state of any man. Even though he may reveal overpowering energy in his momentary activity, it suddenly slackens, he grows forgetful and unreliable. Nor does the unconditional decision reside in the innate character, for the character can be transformed in rebirth. Nor does it reside in what we call in mythological terms a man's demon, for this demon is without loyalty. Overpowering as it may be, no mode of passion, of vital will, of self-assertion, is unconditional in the moment; all are relative and hence perishable.

Thus the unconditional demands an existential decision that has passed through reflection. This means that it does not arise from any natural state but out of freedom, which cannot help being what it is,

56

not because of any natural law but because of its foundation in transcendence.

It is the unconditional which decides the ultimate basis of a man's life, which determines whether it is significant or meaningless. The unconditional is hidden, only in extreme situations does it by silent decision determine a man's road; it is never positively demonstrable, though it always sustains life through existence and can be infinitely elucidated.

Just as trees sink their roots deeply and grow high in the air, so is the fulfilled man rooted in the unconditional; all others are like shrubs which can be pulled up and transplanted, which are interchangeable and in the mass indestructible. But this metaphor is inappropriate, since man arrives at his unconditional foundation not by degrees but by a leap into another dimension.

Second: The unconditional imperative has reality in the man who follows it in faith and awareness.

It cannot be proved, cannot be shown to exist empirically in the world—historical proofs are mere intimations. What we know is always conditional. The unconditional within us has no existence if we apply the yardstick of demonstrable knowledge. A demonstrated unconditional is merely a powerful force, a fanaticism, a frenzy or a madness. If it is asked whether there is any authentic unconditional in the world, the sceptical answer carries universal force of conviction.

For example: it is doubtful whether there is unconditional love, which is rooted in the eternal foundation and does not merely consist in human inclination, passion, habit, and fidelity to a promise. The possibility of authentic communication in loving contest can be denied. That which is demonstrable is by that same token not unconditional.

Third: The unconditional is timeless in time.

The unconditional imperative is not given like empirical existence. It grows within man in time. Only when man conquers himself and goes where his decision unerringly leads him does the unconditional come into its own. Steadfastness of purpose, abstract singlemindedness, mere perseverance in man are not convincing signs that he lives by the unconditional imperative.

In our temporal existence the unconditional attitude is manifested in the experience of extreme situations and in situations when we are in danger of becoming untrue to ourselves.

But the unconditional itself is never entirely temporal. Whenever it may be, it also cuts across time. Regardless of when it is conquered, it is eternal, existing in every new moment through recurrent rebirth from the source. Hence: Where a development in time seems to have given us possession of it, all can still be betrayed in a moment. Conversely, where a man's past seems to be mere factuality, weighing him down under endless contingencies to the point of annihilation, he can nevertheless at any moment begin as it were from the beginning through sudden awareness of the unconditional.

These propositions, it is true, suggest the meaning of the unconditional imperative but do not elucidate its content, which becomes clear only through the antithesis of good and evil.

In heeding the command of the unconditional we effect a choice. A decision becomes the substance of the man. He has chosen what he understands as the good in the decision between good and evil.

Good and evil are differentiated on three levels.

1. We regard as evil the immediate and unrestrained surrender to passions and sensual impulses, to the pleasure and happiness of this world, to empirical existence as such; in short, evil is the life of the man who remains in the sphere of the contingent, who merely lives from day to day like an animal, well or badly, in the unrest of change—a life in which there is no decision.

Good in contradistinction is the life of the man who does not reject the happiness of this world but subordinates it to the morally admissible, seen as the universal law of just action. This morally admissible is the absolute.

2. True evil, as distinguished from mere weakness, which surrenders to the natural bent, consists in what Kant called perversion: I do good only if it does me no harm or does not cost me too much; or stated abstractly: although I will the unconditional embodied in the moral imperative, I follow the law of the good only in so far as it is compatible with undisturbed sensual pleasure; only on this condition, and in no unconditional sense, do I wish to be good. This pseudo-virtue might be called a luxury of fortunate circumstances in which I can afford to be good. In the case of conflict between moral imperative and my vital interest, I may,

according to the magnitude of this interest, be secretly capable of any villainy. In order to avert my own death, I may obey orders to commit murder. Or I may allow my favoured position which saves me from conflict to blind me to my evil.

It is good, in contradistinction, to lift oneself out of this condition of contingency, wherein the unconditional is subordinated to the requirements of vital happiness, and return to an authentic life in the unconditional. This is a conversion from continuous selfbetrayal and impurity of motives to the seriousness of the unconditional.

3. On this level, evil is only the will to evil—the will to destruction as such, the urge to inflict torture, cruelty, annihilation, the nihilistic will to ruin everything that is and has value.

Good, in contradistinction, is the unconditional, which is love and hence the will to reality.

Let us compare these three levels.

On the first level, the relation between good and evil is moral: the question is whether our natural inclinations are governed by a will subservient to moral laws. In Kant's words, duty is opposed to inclination.

On the second level, the relation is ethical: the essential is the authenticity of our motives. The purity of the unconditional is opposed to an impurity which consists in the reversal of the relation of contingency, in which the unconditional is made contingent on practical conditions.

On the third level, the relation becomes metaphysical: here the essential lies in the motives themselves. Love is opposed to hate. Love impels to being, hate to nonbeing. Love grows in bond with transcendence; hate, severed from transcendence, dwindles into the abstract punctuality of the ego. Love works as a quiet building in the world; hate as a loud catastrophe, submerging being in empirical existence and destroying empirical existence itself.

On each level an alternative is revealed, a decision is called for. A man can only want one thing or the other, if he is authentic. He follows inclination or duty, he lives in perversion or in purity of motive, he lives out of hate or out of love. But he can fail to decide. Instead of deciding, we vacillate and stumble through life, combine the one with the other and even accept such a state of things as a necessary contradiction. This indecision is in itself evil. Man awakens only when he distinguishes between good and evil. He becomes himself when he decides which way he is going and acts accordingly. We must all continuously recapture ourselves from indecision. We are so little capable of fulfilling ourselves in goodness that the very force of the passions that drive us headlong through life is indispensable to the lucidity of duty; when we really love we cannot help hating whatever threatens our love; and it is precisely when we feel certain that our motives are pure that we succumb to the perversion of impurity.

The decision has its special character on each of the three levels. Morally, man seeks to base his decision on thought. Ethically, he rehabilitates himself from perversion through a rebirth of his good will. Metaphysically, he achieves awareness of being given to himself in his ability to love. He chooses the right, his motives become authentic, he lives out of love. Only when the three levels become one is the unconditional realized.

To live out of love seems to include all the rest. True love gives certainty regarding the ethical truth of its acts. St. Augustine says: Love and do what thou wilt. But it is impossible for us men to live solely by love, this force of the highest level, for we fall constantly into errors and misunderstandings. Hence we must not rely blindly in our love at every moment but must elucidate it. And for the same reason we finite beings need the discipline by which we conquer our passions, and because of the impurity of our motives we require distrust of ourselves. When we feel sure of ourselves, that is precisely when we are going astray.

Only the unconditional character of the good fills mere duties with content, purifies our ethical motives, dissolves the destructive will of hatred.

But the foundation of love, in which the unconditional is grounded, is identical with the will to authentic reality. I want what I love to be. And I cannot perceive what authentically is without loving it.

VI

MAN

WHAT IS MAN? Physiology studies him as body, psychology as soul, sociology as a social being. We know of man as nature, which we investigate as we do the nature of other living creatures, and as history, which we know by the critical sifting of tradition, by an understanding of the purpose pursued by man in his thoughts and actions, and by the elucidation of events on the basis of motives, situations, natural realities. Our study of man has brought us many kinds of knowledge but not the knowledge of man as a whole.

The question rises: Can man be fully apprehended in that which is knowable concerning him? Or is there something above this, namely, freedom, which evades all object knowledge but is always present in him as potentiality?

The truth is that man is accessible to himself in two ways: as object of inquiry, and as existence endowed with a freedom that is inaccessible to inquiry. In the one case man is conceived as object, in the other as the nonobject which man is and of which he becomes aware when he achieves authentic awareness of himself. We cannot exhaust man's being in knowledge of him, we can experience it only in the primal source of our thought and action. Man is fundamentally more than he can know about himself.

We are conscious of our freedom when we recognize imperatives addressed to us. It is up to us
whether we carry them out or evade them. We cannot
seriously deny that we make a decision, by which we
decide concerning ourselves, and that we are responsible.

No one who attempts to deny this can logically
confront other men with an imperative. Once an
accused man in court said he was not to blame because
he was born that way and could not help doing as he
did and could accordingly not be held responsible;
and the good-humoured judge replied that it might be
just as reasonable to say that the judge who sentenced him could do no differently since that was how
he was and he could not help acting in accordance with
the laws.

Once we have achieved awareness of our freedom we
may take a second step toward the apprehension of
ourselves: Man is a being who exists in relation to
God. What does this mean?

We did not create ourselves. Each man can think
that he might possibly not have been. This we have in
common with the animals. But at the same time, where
in our freedom we decide through ourselves and are
not automatically subordinated to a natural law, we
are not through ourselves but by virtue of being given
to ourselves in our freedom. If we do not love, we do
not know what we should do, we cannot force our
freedom. When we decide freely and conceive of our
lives as meaningful, we know that we do not owe
ourselves to ourselves. At the summit of freedom, upon

which our activity seems necessary to us, not through the outward constraint of an inexorable process of natural law but as the inner consent that does not will otherwise, we are aware of ourselves as freely given to ourselves by transcendence. The more authentically free a man is, the greater his certainty of God. When I am authentically free, I am certain that I am not free through myself.

We men are never adequate to ourselves. We press beyond, and we ourselves grow with the depth of our consciousness of God, through which at the same time we apprehend our insignificance.

Man's relation to God is not a quality given by nature. Because it only is in conjunction with freedom, it awakens in the individual only when from his mere vital assertion of life he takes the leap to his self, that is, to the area where, authentically free from the world, he becomes fully open to the world, where he can be independent of the world, because he lives in bond with God. God is for me in the degree to which I authentically exist.

Once again I repeat: Man as an empirical existent in the world is a knowable object. For example: ethnology apprehends him in diverse racial types, psychoanalysis apprehends him in his unconscious and its workings, Marxism as a living creature producing by his labour, who by production dominates nature and achieves social progress and who can ostensibly achieve perfection in both these respects. Yet all such departments of knowledge apprehend something about man, some process which actually takes place, but never man as a whole. When these methods of inquiry lay claim to absolute knowledge of the whole man—and this they have all done—they lose sight of the real man and go far toward extinguishing their proponents' consciousness of man and even their own humanity, the humanity which is freedom and relation to God.

The study of man is of supreme interest, and if pursued in a spirit of scientific criticism, rewarding. If this is done, we know methodically what and how and within what limits we know a thing and how little we know, in terms of what is possible, and how radically inaccessible to this knowledge authentic humanity remains. And we avert the danger of obscuring man by pseudo-knowledge of him.

Once we know the limits of knowledge, we shall entrust ourselves all the more clearly to the guidance which freedom itself offers to our freedom, if it is oriented toward God.

This is the great question of humanity: Whence does man obtain guidance? For it is certain that his life does not flow along like that of the animals from generation to generation, constantly repeating itself in accordance with natural law; man's freedom opens up to him, along with the uncertainty of his being, an opportunity to become that which he can authentically be. It is given to man to work in freedom upon his empirical existence as upon a material. Hence man alone has a history, that is, he does not live only by his biological heritage but also by tradition. Man's life is not merely a natural process. And his freedom calls for guidance.

We shall not discuss here the cases in which the power of man over man becomes a substitute for this guidance. What we have in mind is the ultimate guidance of man. The thesis of philosophical faith is: Man can live by God's guidance. What does this mean?

We believe that we have in the unconditional imperative an intimation of God's guidance. But how is this possible when God is not corporeal, when there is no unmistakable form in which he exists as God? If God lends guidance, how does man know what God wills? Is there an encounter between man and God? And if so, how does it occur?

We have autobiographical records telling us how, in men faced by critical problems, long doubt has suddenly given way to certainty. This certainty is the freedom to act after perplexity and vacillation. But the freer man knows himself to be in this lucid certainty, the more aware he becomes of the transcendence through which he is.

Kierkegaard reflected each day upon God's guidance, and in such a way that he knew himself to be always in God's hand: through that which he did and that which happened to him in the world he heard God and yet in everything he heard he found many meanings. The guidance he received was not tangible, it provided no clear command; it was guidance through freedom itself, which knows decision because it knows itself rooted in the transcendent foundation.

Guidance through transcendence is different from any guidance in the world, for God's guidance is of only one kind. It is given through freedom itself.

The voice of God lies in the self-awareness that dawns in the individual, when he is open to everything that comes to him from his tradition and environment.

The medium in which man is guided is his judgment regarding his own actions. This judgment restrains or impels, corrects or confirms. The voice of God as judgment regarding man's actions has no other expression in time than in this judgment of man himself with regard to his emotions, motives, actions. In the free and forthright self-awareness of judgment, in self-accusation, in self-affirmation man indirectly finds God's judgment, which is never definitive and always equivocal.

Consequently, human judgment is in error from the outset when man expects to find in it God's final word, upon which he can absolutely rely. We must mercilessly unmask the self-will that lies in our moral self-satisfaction and self-righteousness.

Actually no man can ever be fully and definitively satisfied with himself; he cannot be entirely self-contained in his judgment of himself. He requires the judgment of his fellow men concerning his actions. He is particularly sensitive to the judgment of those he respects. He is less moved by that of the average man and the crowd, of inert individualized institutions, but even here he is not indifferent. Yet the judgment that is ultimately decisive for him is not even that of the men he respects, although this is the only judgment accessible in the world; only the judgment of God can be decisive.

The individual is never entirely independent in his judgment of himself. He always attaches importance to the judgment of another. Even the primitive hero, going to his death in unswerving fortitude, has in mind the judgment of other men: undying fame is the consolation of the dying heroes of the Eddas.

But there is also a truly solitary heroism, which is not based on the community and has no eye to fame. This authentic independence is sustained perhaps by the inner harmony of a well-favoured nature, it draws perhaps unconsciously from the historical tradition of a remembered community, yet its consciousness finds nothing in the present world to which it can hold. But if this heroism does not sink into nothingness, it may be presumed to have deep roots in authentic being, and this, stated explicitly, would be the judgment of God rather than of men.

Though the truth of the judgment by which man is guided is manifested only through self-conviction, this takes two forms: the *universal imperative* and the *historical injunction*.

The universal ethical imperatives carry intuitive conviction. Ever since the ten commandments they have been a form of God's presence. These imperatives can indeed be recognized and followed without faith in God, by a drastic limitation of their meaning to what man can do out of himself. But whole-hearted obedience to the ethical commandment that is clearly heard in freedom is usually bound up with the perception of transcendence precisely in this freedom.

However, action in concrete situations cannot adequately be derived from universal commandments and prohibitions. In every historically actual situation guidance lies in an immediate necessity-of-doing-so, which cannot be derived. But what the individual in this case perceives as his duty remains questionable, however certain he may be of it in his own mind. The very nature of this hearkening to God's guidance implies the risk of error, hence humility. This excludes reliance on our certainty, forbids us to generalize our own acts as an imperative for all, and bars the way to fanaticism. Even the purest clarity as to the road we have seen under God's guidance must not therefore give rise to a certainty that this is the only true road for all.

For it is always possible that everything will look entirely different later. In all lucidity we can choose a false road. Even the certainty of decision, in so far as it is manifested in the world, must retain a certain element of suspension. For the most devastating threat to truth in the world is the overweening claim to the absolutely true. In the certainty of the moment the humility of the enduring question is indispensable.

Only in retrospect are we filled with the wonder of an unfathomable guidance. But even here it carries no certainty, God's guidance cannot be made into a possession.

Psychologically speaking, the voice of God can be heard only in sublime moments. It is out of such moments and toward such moments that we live.

If man experiences guidance through transcendence, is transcendence real for him? What is his relation to it?

Even in the bareness of abstraction, our relation to transcendence can take on a crucial seriousness. But as men in our world we seek support for our certainty in the concrete. Man's supreme achievement in this world is communication from personality to personality. Accordingly, our relation to transcendence, if we may speak in paradox, becomes sensibly present in our encounter with the personal God. The godhead is drawn to us in its aspect of personality, while at the same time we raise ourselves to the level of beings capable of speaking with this God.

In the world, those powers which have flung us to the ground strive to dominate us: fear of the future, anxious attachment to present possessions, care in the face of dire possibilities. [Opposing them man can perhaps in the face of death gain a confidence which will enable him, even in the most extreme, inexplicable, meaningless situation, to die in peace.]

Trust in the foundation of being can manifest itself as disinterested gratitude, as peace in the belief in God's being.

In life, freedom gives us a sense of receiving help from transcendence.

For polytheism, helpers and adversaries become gods and demons. "A god did it" expresses the polytheist's consciousness of events and his own actions, which are thereby hallowed and endowed with significance but at the same time dispersed into innumerable vital and spiritual powers, conceived as existents.

As against this, God's help, in the authentic selfhood that knows itself to be radically dependent, is the help of the One. If God is, there are no demons.

Often God's help is narrowed to a finite content and thus lost. As for example when prayer—as encounter with the invisible God—degenerates from quiet contemplation tending towards silence, succumbs to the passion of seeking the hand of the personal God, and becomes an invocation of this God for practical ends.

To the man who sees through the opaqueness of life God sends all possibilities, including the situations of hopeless annihilation. Then every situation becomes a task for man's freedom, and in this task he stands, grows, and falls. The task, however, cannot be adequately defined as pursuit of earthly happiness but can only be understood clearly through transcendence, this sole reality, and the unconditional commandment of love that is manifested in it, which, infinitely open by virtue of its reason, sees what is and reads the symbols of transcendence in the realities of the world.

Priests, it is true, accuse the individual who orients himself to God through philosophy of arrogance and self-will. They demand obedience to the revealed God. In reply to them this may be said: the individual engaged in philosophical thought, if he has drawn a decision from the primal source, believes that he is obeying God, not with any objective guarantee that he knows God's will but rather as a continuous venture. God works through the free decisions of the individual.

The priests mistake for obedience to God, obedience to such worldly authorities as the Church, books, and laws, which they look upon as direct revelation.

Finally, a true coincidence between obedience to objective authorities in the world and to the originally experienced will of God is possible. But such coincidence must be conquered.

Those who invoke the will of God as experienced by the individual in opposition to objective authorities are misled into an arbitrary refusal to test their experience by the universal and social. But those who conversely invoke objective authority against the will of God as experienced by the individual are beguiled into evasion of the venture to obey God even against the objective authorities, by listening to His will as it speaks from reality itself.

There is an element of helplessness in grasping at the support of reliable laws and authoritative commands. In contradistinction, there is a soaring energy in the individual responsibility of listening to the whole of reality.

A man's humanity depends on how deeply he gains guidance through this listening.

To be a man is to become a man.

VII

THE WORLD

We call reality that which is present to us in practice, that which in our dealings with things, with living creatures, and with men is resistance or becomes matter. We learn to know reality through our daily association with people, through the handling of tools, through technical knowledge, through contact with organized bodies of men.

That which is encountered in practice is clarified by scientific knowledge, and as knowledge of reality made available for new practice.

But by its very nature the knowledge of reality transcends the immediate interests of practical life. Practice, which is always at the same time struggle, mastery of resistance, is only one of its sources. Man wants to know what is real, regardless of any practical interest. A profounder source of the sciences is pure, devoted contemplation, lucid passion, a listening for the world's answers.

Knowledge becomes scientific through method, a systematic unity is ascertained in what is known; the scientist looks beyond the multiple and disparate to unifying principles.

This knowledge of reality seems to find completion in the world system. The world system purports to disclose reality as a whole in one world, a cosmos, every part of which is related to every other part. Though it has always been recognized that such a system must be imperfect and will require constant correction, nevertheless the world system has been regarded as a product of knowledge, and in principle as the form in which being as total reality becomes accessible to us. The world system is expected to encompass the whole of coherent knowledge. World systems are as old as human knowledge; and thinkers at all times have striven for world systems as a means of attaining a unified awareness of the whole.

Now it is significant that the search for an all-embracing world system, in which the universe becomes a self-contained whole, this so self-evident striving for a total world view, is based on a fundamental fallacy which has only been understood in recent times.

For scientific critique teaches us not only that every world system up to now has collapsed under the weight of its own contradictions but that the systematic unities of knowledge which are indeed the goal of science have been diverse and sprung from essentially different roots. This becomes increasingly evident with the advance of science. Even as the unities become more universal—particularly in physics—the more marked become the cleavages between the physical world, the world of life, the world of the soul, the world of the mind. These worlds are indeed connected. They are arranged in an order of development; the reality of the later stage presupposes that of the earlier, while the reality of the earlier seems able to stand without that of the later; for example, there can be no life without matter but there can be matter without life. Vain attempts have been made to derive the later stage from the earlier, but always the gap becomes more evident. The one totality in the world, to which all the unities susceptible of exploration by knowledge belong, is itself no unity such as might be subsumed in an all-embracing theory, or which as idea might serve as a beacon for scientific inquiry. There is no world system but only a systematization of the sciences.

World systems are always a particular sphere of knowledge, erroneously absolutized and universalized. Different scientific ideas give rise to special perspectives. Every world system is a segment taken out of the world. The world itself cannot become a system. All "scientific cosmologies" have been mythical cosmologies, built on scientific methods and scant remnants of myth.

The world is no object, we are always in the world, we confront objects in it but never have the world itself as an object. Far as our horizons of methodical inquiry extend, particularly in our astronomical conceptions of the nebulae, of which our Galaxy, with its billions of suns, is only one among millions, and in the mathematical conception of universal matter, all that we see here is aspects of phenomena and not the foundation of things, not the universe as a whole.

The universe is not self-contained. It cannot be explained out of itself, but in it one thing can be explained by another ad infinitum. No one knows to what limits future research may yet attain, what abysses will still open before it.

A critical approach to science calls for the abandonment of world systems, which is also a prerequisite to any philosophical apperception of being. True, the philosophical quest of being demands a familiarity with every branch of scientific inquiry. But it seems to be the hidden aim of science to attain through inquiry to a limit at which the area of nonknowledge is opened to the most lucid knowledge. For only fulfilled knowledge can lead to authentic nonknowledge. Then authentic being is revealed not in any world system built on knowledge but in fulfilled nonknowledge, which can be achieved only through scientific cognition, not without it and not before it. It is the supreme striving of knowledge to reach the point where cognition fails. For our consciousness of being finds an indispensable source in nonknowledge, but only in fulfilled, conquered nonknowledge.

We approach the reality of the world from a different angle. Scientific knowledge can be included in the general proposition: All knowledge is interpretation. The method we apply to the study of texts may be taken as a parallel to our study of being. And the analogy is not accidental.

For we possess being only in its interpretations. To speak of it is to interpret it, and only that which is apprehended in speech falls under the head of the knowable. But even in the prephilosophic stage the language of men's practical dealings with things contains an interpretation of being; being is always defined in reference to something else. Being is for us only in an interpretive context. Being and the knowledge of being, the existent and what we say of it, are accordingly a texture of diverse interpretations. All being is for us an interpretation.

Interpretation differentiates between something that is and something which it means, for example, between the sign and what it stands for. If being is taken as that which is to be interpreted, it would seem that we must differentiate in the same way: interpretation concerns something other than itself; what confronts us in interpretation is being itself. But our attempted differentiation is not successful. For nothing enduring remains, nothing purely knowable, which need only be interpreted and is not itself interpretation. Whatever we know is only a beam of light cast by our interpretation into being, or, we might say, the capture of an opportunity for interpretation. The power to make possible all these interpretations must lie in the very nature of being as a whole.

But the interpretation is not arbitrary. If it is sound, it has an objective character. Being compels these interpretations. True, all modes of being are for us modes of interpretation, but they are also modes of necessary interpretation. Consequently, the doctrine of the categories as structures of being sees the modes of being as modes of interpretation, thus for example breaking down the "objective" categories into identity, relation, cause and effect, freedom or expression, etc.

To us all being in its interpretations is like a reflection spreading out in all directions.

The modes of reality are also modes of interpretation. Interpretation implies that the text is not in itself the reality of being but a mode in which being is manifested. Absolute reality cannot be apprehended by any interpretation. It is always a perversion of our knowledge when the content of an interpretation is looked upon as reality itself.

Fundamentally we can express the reality of the world as the *phenomenality* of empirical existence. Everything we have said thus far: that there is an element of suspension in all modes of reality; that world systems represent merely relative perspectives; that knowledge has the character of interpretation; that being is manifested in the dichotomy of subject and object—our whole characterization of the knowledge to which man can attain—implies that objects are mere appearances; no being that we know is being in itself and as a whole. The phenomenality of the empirical world was made fully clear by Kant. Though it is not subject to compelling knowledge, because it cannot be perceived objectively but only by a transcending, nevertheless it imposes itself on every intellect that is capable of transcendence. And then it does not add a new particular knowledge to the knowledges we had before, but effects a shift in our whole consciousness of being. Hence the sudden but enduring light which is kindled in the philosophical approach to the reality of the world. If the light is not kindled, the propositions of philosophy remain unfulfilled and hence fundamentally not understood.

It is not only the absolute world systems that are gone. The world is not self-contained and for our knowledge it breaks down into diverse perspectives, because it cannot be reduced to a single principle. The reality of the world as a whole is no object of knowledge.

In the light of what we have said of God and existence, we may sum up our experience of the world in the proposition: The reality of the world subsists ephemerally between God and existence.

Everyday life seems to teach us the contrary: that we men take the world or something in the world as an absolute. And of the man who has made so many things the ultimate content of his existence we may say with Luther: that which you hold to, upon which you stake your existence, that is truly your God. Man cannot help taking something as an absolute, whether willingly and knowingly, whether accidentally and fitfully or resolutely and steadfastly. Man has a kind of home in the absolute. He cannot evade it. In that home he must live.

History down through the centuries reveals awe-inspiring figures of men who have transcended the world. Indian ascetics, certain monks in China and the West, left the world in order to partake of the absolute in worldless meditation. It was as though the world had vanished; being—from the viewpoint of the world, nothingness—was everything.

Chinese mystics freed themselves from the toils of

worldly desire and rose to heights of pure contemplation in which the world became speech, transparent, ephemeral manifestation of the Eternal, infinite omnipresence of its law. For them, time was dissolved in eternity, and the world spoke to them in the eternal present.

There have been Western scientists, philosophers, poets, and some few men of action who have passed through the world as though, despite their firm attachment to the world, they retained permanent roots outside it. Coming from a distant home, they found themselves and things in the world, and while remaining close to things, they transcended the temporal manifestation in favour of their memory of the eternal.

We others, who are chained to the world, who have not found that foundation in being with the clear certainty of practical life and knowledge, tend to assess the world:

In happy situations, the magic of worldly fulfilment beguiles us into seeing the world as a harmony of being. But when we experience evil and horror and despair in the face of this reality, we rebel. To the harmony of being we defiantly juxtapose nihilism in the proposition: All is absurdity.

Honesty must recognize the untruth both in the ideas of harmony of being and nihilistic chaos. Both embody a total judgment and that total judgment concerning the world and things rests upon inadequate knowledge. It is incumbent upon man to reject the fixation of conflicting total judgments, in lasting willingness to listen to event, destiny, and his own acts in the temporal course of his life. This willingness implies two fundamental experiences:

First the experience of God's absolute transcendence over the world: the hidden God recedes farther and farther into the distance if I attempt to seize and apprehend Him universally and forever; He is incalculably near through the absolutely historical form of His speech in a situation which is always unique.

Second, the experience of God's speech in the world: the world is not in itself, but in it God speaks, always with many meanings, and this speech can only become clear historically in the existential moment and cannot be generalized.

Freedom for being does not see the ultimate in the world as such. In the world eternal being and temporal manifestation meet.

Yet we do not experience eternal being outside of that which is empirically manifested to us in time. Since that which is for us must be manifested in the temporality of the world, there can be no direct knowledge of God and existence. There can only be faith.

The principles of faith—God is; there is an unconditional imperative; man is finite and imperfectible; man can live in God's guidance—enable us to sense the truth only in so far as they embody their fulfilment in the world as speech of God. If, as though passing the world by, God should directly approach existence, the event would be incommunicable. The truth of all universal principles speaks in the form of a tradition and of a particularity acquired in life; these are the forms in which the individual consciousness has awakened to the truth: our parents told us so. There is a vast historical depth in such formulas as "for Thy Holy name's sake," "immortality," "love."

As principles of faith become more universal they lose their historicity. They rise to the level of pure abstraction. But with such abstractions alone no man can live; where concrete fulfilment is lacking they retain only a minimal value as guides to memory and hope. They have at the same time a cleansing power: they free us from the fetters of pure materiality and from superstitious narrowness, helping us to adapt the great tradition to present realization.

Unlimited devotion to God is the authentic mode of existence. That to which I devote myself in the world, to the point of staking my life, must be constantly tested in relation to God, under the condition of God's will in which we believe. For in blind devotion man heedlessly serves the power which is over him only factually and which he does not elucidate, and he may even serve the "devil" through his failure to see, question, think.

In devotion to reality in the world—the indispensable medium of devotion to God—grows selfhood, which at the same time asserts itself in that to which it is devoted. But if all empirical existence has been reduced to reality, family, people, profession, state, world, and if this reality fails, then we can conquer the despair of nothingness only through the self-assertion which transcends the reality of the world, which stands alone before God and exists out of God. Only in devotion to

God and not to the world is this selfhood granted and received as the freedom to assert it in the world.

The ephemeral subsistence of the world between God and existence is the burden of a myth which—in biblical categories—conceives the world as the manifestation of a transcendent history: from the creation through the fall of man and the redemption to the end of the world and the resurrection of all things. In this myth the world does not exist out of itself but is a passing stage in a transcendent process. The world is transient, but the reality in this transience is God and existence. The eternal is manifested in the time of the world. It is thus that man as an individual has knowledge of himself. And in this manifestation of the eternal there lies a paradox: for in it that which is eternal as such is once again decided.

VIII

FAITH AND ENLIGHTENMENT

WE HAVE STATED the principles of philosophical faith: God is; there is an unconditional imperative; man is finite and imperfectible; man can live in God's guidance; the reality of the world subsists ephemerally between God and existence. These five propositions reinforce and lend impetus to one another. But each has its own source in a fundamental experience of existence.

None of these five principles is demonstrable in the sense of a limited insight into objects in the world. Their truth can only be "pointed out," "elucidated" by a chain of reasoning, "recalled to mind." They do not constitute a creed, for despite the force of the faith that is placed in them they remain in the suspension of nonknowledge. I follow them not because I accept a dogma in obedience to an authority but because by my very nature I cannot elude their truth.

Glib statements of principles fill us with misgiving. They are too readily treated like a body of knowledge, and this vitiates their purpose. They are too readily made into a dogma which is substituted for reality. They should be communicated, in order that men may understand one another through them, in order that they may be confirmed by communication, in order that they may awaken men when conditions are favourable. But by the definiteness of their statement they give rise to pseudo-knowledge.

Statement demands discussion. For when we think, there are always two possibilities: we may arrive at the truth or we may miss it. Thus every positive statement demands safeguards against error, and side by side with the ordered building up of thought we find perversion. Consequently, all positive exposition must be permeated by negative judgments, limitation, and critique. But in philosophical thought this battle of discussion is not a struggle for power; it is a struggle for lucidity through questioning, a struggle for clarity and truth, in which we allow our adversary all those weapons of the intellect with which we defend our own faith.

In philosophizing I have recourse to direct statement where a direct question is asked. Is there a God? Is there an unconditional imperative in our life? Is man imperfectible? Is there guidance by God? Is the reality of the world suspended and ephemeral? I am compelled to answer, when I am confronted by the principles characterizing lack of faith, which are more or less as follows:

First: There is no God, for there is only the world and the laws governing its process; the world is God.

Second: There is no unconditional imperative, for the imperatives which I obey originated in time and are in process of change. They are determined by custom, habit, tradition, obedience; everything is contingent upon something else ad infinitum.

Third: Man is perfectible, for man can be just as perfect in his way as the animal; it will be possible to breed a perfect man. There is no inherent, fundamental imperfection or frailty in man. Man is no intermediate being but complete and whole. True, like everything else in the world he is transient, but he is grounded in himself, independent, adequate to himself in his world.

Fourth: There is no guidance by God. This guidance is an illusion and a self-deception. Man has the strength to follow himself and can rely on his own strength.

Fifth: The world is everything, its reality is the sole and authentic reality. Since there is no transcendence, everything in the world is indeed transient, but the world itself is absolute, it is eternal and not ephemeral, it is not transition and suspension.

In dealing with such statements of lack of faith philosophy has a twofold task: to apprehend their origin and to elucidate the truth of faith.

Lack of faith is generally regarded as a product of the Enlightenment. But what is enlightenment?*

The teachings of enlightenment are directed against the blindness which accepts ideas as true without questioning them; against actions—e.g., magical actions—which cannot accomplish what they are expected to accomplish, since belief in their efficacy is based on assumptions which can be proved false; against restrictions on questioning and inquiry; against traditional prejudices. Enlightenment demands an unlimited striving for insight and a critical awareness of the quality and limit of every insight.

* It is clear in Jaspers' discussion of the enlightenment that he is not primarily concerned with the historical movement known as *the* Enlightenment. As a perennially significant philosophical attitude, enlightenment is opposed to superstition, prejudice, and anything else that obstructs the deepest apprehension of and response to reality.

Man strives to understand what he believes, desires, and does. He wants to think for himself. He wishes to grasp with his understanding, and where possible to have proof of what is true. He wants his knowledge to be based on experience which is fundamentally accessible to everyone. He seeks paths to the source of insight instead of permitting it to be set before him as a finished product which he need only accept. He wishes to understand to what degree a proof is valid and at what limits the understanding is frustrated. And he would like also to have a reasoned basis for the indemonstrable premise, which he must ultimately take as the foundation of his life, of the authority he follows, of the veneration he feels, of the respect in which he holds the thoughts and actions of great men, of the trust which he places in something which, whether only at this particular time and in this particular situation or in general, is unfathomed and unfathomable. Even in obedience he wants to know why he obeys. He subjects everything he holds to be true and everything that he does in the belief that it is right to this condition; he himself must participate in it inwardly. And such participation must be based on self-conviction. In short: enlightenment is—in the words of Kant—"man's departure from the condition of immaturity for which he himself is responsible." In truth it is the path by which man comes to himself.

But the demands of enlightenment are so easily misunderstood that the very term is ambivalent. There can be true and there can be false enlightenment. And accordingly the fight against enlightenment is itself ambivalent. It can—rightly—be directed against false, or—unjustifiably—be directed against true enlightenment. Often the two are mingled in one.

Enemies of the Enlightenment have said that it destroyed the tradition upon which all life rested; that it dissolved faith and led to nihilism; that it gave to each man the freedom of his arbitrary will, thus producing disorder and anarchy; that it made men wretched by destroying their roots.

These accusations apply to a false enlightenment which itself has ceased to understand the nature of true enlightenment. False enlightenment strives to base all knowledge and will and action upon mere understanding (instead of merely using the understanding as an indispensable means of elucidating that which must be given to it); it absolutizes the insights of the understanding, which are always particular (instead of merely applying them to the sphere that is appropriate to them); it misleads the individual into asserting that he can know by himself alone and that he can act on the basis of his knowledge alone, as though the individual were everything (instead of basing himself upon the living context of the knowledge obtained through questioning and searching in common with other men); it lacks the feeling for exception and authority, by which all human life must orient itself. In short, it strives to stand man upon himself, in the belief that he can attain to everything that is true and essential through intellectual insight. It strives only to know and not to believe.

True enlightenment on the other hand, while it does not from outside, by intention and coercion, impose a limit upon questioning, is aware of the factual limit. For it not only elucidates prejudices and common beliefs which were hitherto unquestioned but also elucidates itself. It does not confound the methods of the understanding with the contents of humanity. In its view these contents can be elucidated by rational understanding but they cannot be based upon the understanding.

Let us now discuss some of the attacks that have been made on enlightenment. It has been called the super-erogation of man, who wishes to owe only to himself what has been bestowed upon him by grace.

Those who make this accusation fail to recognize that God does not speak through the commands and revelations of other men but in man's selfhood and through his freedom, not from without but from within. Any restriction on man's freedom, created by God and oriented toward God, is a restriction upon the very thing through which God manifests himself. The enemies of enlightenment rebel against God himself in favour of supposedly divine but actually manmade contents of faith, injunctions, prohibitions, institutions and rules of conduct, wherein, as in all things human, folly and wisdom are inextricably intermingled. To cease questioning these things is to renounce the human mission. The rejection of enlightenment is a kind of treason against man.

One of the main elements of enlightenment is *science*, a science free from preconceived notions, whose searching and questioning are not limited by aims and truths set forth in advance (apart from such ethical, humanitarian restrictions as those forbidding the use of men as objects of experiment).

We have heard the outcry: Science destroys faith. Greek science could be built into faith and was useful for its elucidation, but modern science is utterly ruinous. It is a purely historical phenomenon resulting from a catastrophic world crisis. We may expect its end and should do our utmost to hasten it. These critics doubt the eternal truth which shines forth in modern science. They deny the dignity of man which is today no longer possible without a scientific attitude. They attack philosophical enlightenment, which they associate only with the flatness of the understanding and not with the breadth of reason. They turn against liberalism, seeing only the congealed liberalism of laissez faire and superficial faith in progress, not the profound force of liberality. They attack tolerance as heartless indifference, and fail to recognize the universal human readiness for communication. In short they reject our foundation in human dignity, in the power to attain knowledge, in freedom, and advocate philosophical suicide.

In opposition to these beliefs we are certain that today there can be no integrity, reason, or human dignity without a true scientific attitude, where tradition and situation make this attitude possible. Where science is lost man falls into the twilight of vaguely edifying sentiments, of fanatical decisions arrived at in self-willed blindness. Barriers are erected, man is led into new prisons.

Why these attacks on enlightenment?
Not infrequently they grow out of an urge to

absurdity, a drive to set men up as mouthpieces of God and obey them. They arise out of passion for the night, which no longer follows the laws of the day but amid the experience of the bottomless builds a supposedly saving pseudo-order without foundation. And they grow out of the unfaith of those who, in their desire for faith, persuade themselves that they have a faith. And out of a will to power which fosters the belief that men are more compliant when they are blindly subservient to an authority which is an instrument of this power.

Often the enemies of enlightenment have invoked Christ and the New Testament—rightly so if they had in mind certain churches and theologies down through the centuries, but unjustifiably if they were thinking of the source and truth of the biblical religion as such, for these are alive in true enlightenment, they are elucidated by philosophy, which helps perhaps to preserve them for humanity in the new technological world.

If the attacks on enlightenment often seem meaningful, it is because of the perversions of enlightenment, which are indeed open to attack. What makes the perversions possible is the difficulty of the task. It is true that the enthusiasm with which every newly awakening man attains freedom and through it a greater sense of openness to the godhead goes hand in hand with enlightenment. But soon enlightenment may become an unwarranted aspiration. For God is not heard unequivocally out of freedom but only in the course of lifelong effort through moments when man is granted what he could never attain by thought. Men cannot always bear the burden of critical non-knowledge in mere readiness to listen at the proper moment. He desires definite knowledge of the ultimate.

Once he has rejected faith, he abandons himself to the intellect as such, and from it falsely expects certainty in the decisive questions of life. But since thought cannot provide such certainty, his expectations can be fulfilled only by deceptions: the finite and determinate, sometimes this, sometimes that, and so on in endless variations, is absolutized into the whole. A particular category is taken for cognition as such. The continuity of persevering self-examination gives way to overweening trust in a definitive pseudo-certainty. Men claim absolute truth for opinions based on accident and situation, and in their pseudo-lucidity succumb to a new blindness. In its assertion that man can know and think everything on the basis of his own insight, such enlightenment is indeed arbitrary. It supports this impossible claim by undisciplined half-thinking.

We cannot combat all these perversions of enlightenment by abolishing thought but only by a realization of thought with its full potentialities, with its critical awareness of limits and its valid accomplishments which sustain the test of knowledge. Only a development of thought achieved through the self-education of the whole man can prevent any body of thought whatsoever from becoming a poison; can prevent enlightenment from becoming an agent of death.

The purest enlightenment recognizes that it cannot dispense with faith. The five propositions of philosophical faith cannot be demonstrated like scientific theses. It is not possible to impose faith by rational means, by any science or philosophy.

It is a fallacy of false enlightenment to suppose that the understanding by itself alone can know truth and being. The understanding is dependent on something else. As scientific cognition, it is dependent on sensory experience. As philosophy, it is dependent on contents of faith.

The understanding can indeed clarify, purify, develop thought, but that which lends its opinions objective significance, its thought fulfilment, its action purpose, its philosophy authentic content must be given to it.

The source of these premises upon which thought must depend is ultimately unknowable. They are rooted in the Comprehensive out of which we live. If the force of the Comprehensive fails us, we incline to the five negative propositions of unfaith.

The premises of sensory experience come from the world, the premises of faith have their source in historical tradition. In this outward form the premises are merely guides by which we find our way to the authentic premises. For the outward premises are subject to constant testing, not only by the understanding as a judge who of himself knows what is true but by the understanding as an instrument: the understanding tests experience by other experience; it also tests traditional faith by traditional faith, and in so doing tests all tradition by the original awakening of its contents out of the primal source of our own selfhood. The sciences provide those necessary insights into experience which no one following the prescribed methods can elude; while philosophy, through its reasoned approach to tradition, makes possible our faith.

We cannot combat unfaith directly but we can combat the demonstrably false claims of rationalistic pseudo-knowledge and the claims of faith that assume a falsely rational form.

The principles of philosophical faith become false when they are taken as communication of a content. For none of these principles implies an absolute object; they are to be taken as the symbol of an infinity becoming concrete. Where this infinity is present in faith, the endless reality of the world takes on meaning as its manifestation. But this meaning must still be interpreted.

When the philosopher utters these principles of faith, they assume an analogy to a creed. The philosopher should not exploit his nonknowledge in order to evade all answers. He must be circumspect in his philosophizing and repeat: I do not know; I do not even know whether I believe; however, such faith, expressed in such propositions, strikes me as meaningful; I will venture to believe in this way, and I hope I shall have the strength to live by my faith. In philosophy there will always be a tension between the seeming indecision of the suspended utterance and the reality of resolute conduct.

IX

THE HISTORY OF MAN*

No reality is more essential to our self-awareness than history. It shows us the broadest horizon of mankind, brings us the contents of tradition upon which our life is built, shows us standards by which to measure the present, frees us from unconscious bondage to our own age, teaches us to see man in his highest potentialities and his imperishable creations.

We can make no better use of leisure than to familiarize ourselves and keep ourselves familiar with the glories of the past and the catastrophes in which everything has been shattered. We gain a better understanding of our present experience if we see it in the mirror of history. And history becomes alive for us when we regard it in the light of our own age. Our life becomes richer when past and present illumine one another.

It is only the concrete, particular history which is close to us that truly concerns us. Yet in our philosophical approach to history we inevitably deal in certain abstractions.

History sometimes appears to be a chaos of accidental happenings, an eddying flood. It passes on, from one turmoil, from one catastrophe to the next, with brief intervals of happiness, little islands which it

* In this chapter certain passages from my book *Vom Ursprung und Ziel der Geschichte* have been reproduced verbatim.

spares for a time, until they too are engulfed. All in all
—as Max Weber put it—a road paved by the devil
with demolished values.

True, our insight has revealed certain connections,
causal relations, such as the effects of technological
inventions on working methods, of working methods
on social structures, of conquests on ethnic grouping,
of military technique on military organization and of
military organization on political structure, and so on
ad infinitum. And beyond causality we also find certain
total aspects, as in the succession of cultural styles over
a series of generations, as epochs of culture each rooting
in the one before it, as great self-contained culture-
bodies in their development. Spengler and his followers
saw such cultures growing out of the mass of vegetating
mankind like plants springing from the soil, flowering
and dying, and having little or no bearing upon one
another; Spengler counted eight of them up to our
time, Toynbee twenty-one.

Seen in this way history has no meaning, no unity
and no structure, but reveals only innumerable chains
of causality and morphological organisms such as
occur in the natural process (except that in history
they can be defined with far less precision).

But the philosophy of history implies the search for
meaning, unity, and structure in history. It can deal
only with mankind as a whole.

Let us draw up a brief outline of history.

Men have been living for hundreds of thousands of
years; this is proved by bones found in geological
strata which can be dated. For tens of thousands of
years there have been men exactly like us anatomically,

as is shown by paintings and remains of tools. But it is only for the last five to six thousand years that we have had a documented, coherent history.

History breaks down into four basic segments:

First: We can only infer the first great steps toward the use of language, the invention of tools, the kindling and use of fire. This is the Promethean age, the foundation of all history, through which man became man in distinction to a purely biologically defined human species, of which we can scarcely conceive. When this was, over what vast periods of time the process extended, we do not know. But this age must be situated in the very remote past and it must have been many times longer than the comparatively insignificant span of time covered by our documented historical era.

Second: The ancient high civilizations grew up between 5000 and 3000 B.C. in Egypt, Mesopotamia, and on the Indus, somewhat later on the Hwang River in China. These are little islands of light amid the broad mass of mankind which already populated the whole planet.

Third: In the years centring around 500 B.C.— from 800 to 200—the spiritual foundations of humanity were laid, simultaneously and independently in China, India, Persia, Palestine, and Greece. And these are the foundations upon which humanity still subsists today.

Fourth: Since then there has been only one entirely new, spiritually and materially incisive event, equal to the others in historical significance: the age of science and technology. It was foreshadowed in Europe at the end of the Middle Ages; its theoretical groundwork was laid in the seventeenth century; at the end of the eighteenth century it entered on a period of broad growth, and in the last few decades it has advanced at a headlong pace.

Let us cast a glance at the third segment, that of the years around 500 B.C. Hegel has said, "All history moves toward Christ and from Christ. The appearance of the Son of God is the axis of history." Our calendar reminds us every day of this Christian structure of history. The flaw in this view of history is that it can have meaning only for believing Christians. But even Western Christians have not built their empirical view of history on their faith but have drawn an essential distinction between sacred and profane history.

If there is an axis in history, we must find it empirically in profane history, as a set of circumstances significant for all men, including Christians. It must carry conviction for Westerners, Asiatics, and all men, without the support of any particular content of faith, and thus provide all men with a common historical frame of reference.

The spiritual process which took place between 800 and 200 B.C. seems to constitute such an axis. It was then that the man with whom we live today came into being. Let us designate this period as the "axial age." Extraordinary events are crowded into this period. In China lived Confucius and Lao Tse, all the trends in Chinese philosophy arose, it was the era of Mo Tse, Chuang Tse and countless others. In India it was the age of the Upanishads and of Buddha; as in China, all philosophical trends, including skepticism and materialism, sophistry and nihilism, were developed. In Iran Zarathustra put forward his challenging conception of the cosmic process as a struggle between good and evil; in Palestine prophets arose: Elijah, Isaiah, Jeremiah, Deutero-Isaiah; Greece produced Homer, the philosophers Parmenides, Heraclitus, Plato, the tragic poets, Thucydides, and Archimedes. All the vast development of which these names are a mere intimation took place in these few centuries, independently and almost simultaneously in China, India, and the West.

The new element in this age is that man everywhere became aware of being as a whole, of himself and his limits. He experienced the horror of the world and his own helplessness. He raised radical questions, approached the abyss in his drive for liberation and redemption. And in consciously apprehending his limits he set himself the highest aims. He experienced the absolute in the depth of selfhood and in the clarity of transcendence.

Conflicting possibilities were explored. Discussion, partisanship, intellectual schisms (though within a common frame of reference) gave rise to movement and unrest bordering on spiritual chaos.

This era produced the basic categories in which we still think and created the world religions out of which men still live.

The opinions, customs, conditions which had hitherto enjoyed unconscious acceptance came to be questioned. The world was thrown into turmoil.

The mythical age with its peace of mind and self-evident truths was ended. This was the beginning of the struggle—based on rationality and empirical experience—against the myth; of the battle against the demons for the transcendence of the one God; ethical indignation waged war on false gods. Myths were transformed and infused with deep meaning in the very moment when the myth as such was destroyed.

Man was no longer self-contained. He was uncertain of himself, hence open to new and boundless possibilities.

For the first time there were philosophers. Men dared to stand upon their own feet as individuals. Hermits and wandering thinkers in China, ascetics in India, philosophers in Greece, prophets in Israel may be grouped together, greatly as they differ in faith, ideas, and inner attitude. Man opposed his own inwardness to the whole world. He discovered in himself the primal source, by virtue of which he might rise above himself and the world.

And in that same era man gained awareness of history. It was an age of extraordinary beginnings, but men felt and knew that an infinite past had gone before. Even in this first awakening of the truly human spirit man was sustained by memory, he had consciousness of lateness, even of decadence.

Men strove to plan and control the course of events, to restore desirable conditions or produce them for the first time. Thinkers speculated as to how men might best live together, as to how they might best be administered and governed. It was an age of reform.

And the sociological conditions of all three regions reveal analogies: innumerable petty states and cities, a struggle of all against all, and yet at first an astonishing prosperity.

But these centuries in which so much happened were not characterized by a simple ascending development. There was destruction and creation at once, and there was no fulfilment. The supreme potentialities realized in individuals did not become a common heritage. What started out as freedom of movement became anarchy in the end. Once the era lost its creative impetus, ideas congealed into dogmas and a levelling occurred in all three spheres. As the disorder grew intolerable, men sought new bonds and new stability.

The end was first characterized by political developments. Vast despotic empires arose almost simultaneously in China (Tsin, Shi, Huangti), in India (the Maurya dynasty), in the West (the Hellenistic empires and the Imperium Romanum). Everywhere systematic order and technical organization emerged from the collapse.

The spiritual life of men is still oriented toward the axial age. China, India, and the West have all witnessed conscious attempts to restore it, renaissances. True, there have been great new spiritual creations but they have been inspired by ideas acquired in the axial age.

Thus the main line of history runs from the birth of humanity through the civilizations of high antiquity to the axial age and its offshoots, which played a creative role up to the dawn of our own era.

Since then a new line would seem to have begun. Our age of science and technology is a kind of second beginning, comparable to the first invention of tools and fire-making.

If we may venture a presumption by analogy, we shall pass through vast planned organizations analogous to those of Egypt and the other ancient high civilizations, from which the ancient Jews emigrated and on which, when they laid a new foundation, they looked back with hatred as a place of forced labour. Perhaps mankind will pass through these giant organizations to a new axial age, still remote, invisible, and inconceivable, an axial age of authentic human upsurge.

But today we are living in an era of the most terrible catastrophes. It seems as though everything that had been transmitted to us were being melted down, and yet there is no convincing sign that a new edifice is in the making.

What is new is that in our day history is for the first time becoming world-wide in scope. Measured by the unity which modern communications have given to the globe, all previous history is a mere aggregate of local histories.

What we formerly called history is ended—an intermediary moment of five thousand years between the prehistoric centuries in which the globe was populated and the world history which is now beginning. These millennia, measured by the preceding era of man's existence and by future possibilities, are a minute interval. In this interval men may be said to have gathered together, to have mustered their forces for the action of world history, to have acquired the intellectual and technical equipment they needed for the journey which is just beginning.

We must look to horizons such as these when we incline to take a dark view of the realities of our day and to regard all human history as lost. We are justified in believing in the future potentialities of humanity. In the short view all is gloom, in the long view it is not. But this becomes evident only in the light of history as a whole.

The more fully we realize ourselves in the present, seeking the truth and ascertaining the criteria of humanity, the more confidently we may look to the future.

And now, as to the *meaning* of history. Those who believe that the historical process has an aim often strive to realize it by planning.

But we become aware of our helplessness when we seek to plan and organize history as a whole. The overweening plans of rulers, based upon a supposed total knowledge of history, have always ended in catastrophe. The plans devised by individuals in their restricted circles fail or else contribute to unleashing quite different, unplanned complexes of events. The historical process can be seen either as an irresistible mechanism or as an infinitely interpretable meaning which manifests itself by unexpected new events, which remains always equivocal, a meaning which, even when we entrust ourselves to it, is never known to us.

If we seek the meaning of history in a movement toward some ultimate state of happiness on earth, we find no corroboration in any conceivable view of past history. On the contrary, the whole chaotic course of human history, with its modest successes and total catastrophes, argues against such meaning. The meaning of history cannot be formulated in terms of an aim.

Every aim is particular, provisional, and capable of being transcended. It is only by ignoring essential facts that we can interpret the whole of history as the story of a single decision.

What does God want of men? Perhaps a general answer may be ventured: History is the stage upon which man can reveal what he is, what he can be, what he can become, of what he is capable. Even the greatest threat is a challenge to man. Man's ascent cannot be measured only in terms of security.

But history means far more: it is the stage on which the being of the godhead is revealed. Being is revealed in man through his dealings with other men. For God does not disclose himself in history in any single, exclusive way. Potentially each man stands in immediate relation to God. Amid all the diversity of history we must give the unique, the irreplaceable, its due.

From all this it follows that if I attempt to foresee tangible happiness in the form of perfection on earth, of a human paradise, I can expect nothing; but I can expect everything if I am oriented toward the profound humanity which opens up with faith in God. I can hope for nothing if I look only outward; for everything if, partaking of the primal source, I entrust myself to transcendence.

We cannot define the ultimate aim of history but we can posit an aim which is itself a premise for the realization of the highest human potentialities. And that is the *unity of mankind*.

Unity cannot be achieved through any rational, scientific universal. This would produce a unity of the understanding but not of mankind. Nor does unity reside in a universal religion, such as might be arrived at through discussion at religious congresses. Nor can it be realized through a conventional language based on reason and common sense. Unity can be gained only from the depth of historicity, not as a common, knowable content but in boundless communication of the historically different in never-ending dialogue, rising to heights of noble emulation.

A dialogue of this sort, which will be worthy of man, requires an area of freedom from violence. A practical unity of men striving for such an area of nonviolence seems conceivable, and many have already taken it as their goal. This goal of unifying mankind at least on the basic levels of life, which does not imply a common and universal faith, does not seem entirely utopian. Its realization will require a stubborn political struggle against the powers that be—and our very situation may well drive us into such a struggle.

Prerequisite for such a unity is a political form upon which all can agree, since it provides the best possible basis of freedom for all. This form, which only in the

West has been developed in theory and in part realized, is the constitutional state built on elections and on laws which are subject to modification solely by legal means. In such a state men battle to gain recognition for the just cause, to win public opinion through widespread and enlightened education and the unreserved dissemination of news.

There would be no wars in a constitutional world order where no state would possess absolute sovereignty but mankind itself, acting through its constitutional organs, would be sovereign.

But if humanity desires communication and aspires to end violence through a constitutional order which, though unjust, is moving toward justice, we shall not be helped by an optimism born of enthusiasm for such ideas, which sees the future as all bright. For we have every reason to take the opposite view.

We see, each of us in ourself, the self-will, the resistance to self-elucidation, the sophistry, with which even philosophy is used as an instrument of obfuscation; we see rejection of the unfamiliar in the place of communication. We see the pleasure men take in power and violence; we see how the masses are swept into war; stricken with blind lust for gain and adventure, willing to sacrifice everything, even their lives. On the other hand we see the unwillingness of the masses to deprive themselves, to save, to work patiently and quietly toward the building of stable conditions; and we see the passions which force their way almost unobstructed into the background of the mind.

And quite apart from the character of men, we see the irremediable injustice of all institutions, we see situations which cannot be solved by justice, the situations arising for example from the increase and redistribution of the population or from the exclusive possession by one group of something which all desire and which cannot be divided.

Hence there seems almost to be an inevitable limit at which violence in some form must again break through. Once again we are faced with the question: is it God or the devil who governs the world? And though we may believe that ultimately the devil is in the service of God, there is no proof of it.

When in our isolation we see our lives seeping away as a mere succession of moments, tossed meaninglessly about by accidents and overwhelming events; when we contemplate a history that seems to be at an end, leaving only chaos behind it, then we are impelled to raise ourselves above history.

Yet we must remain aware of our epoch and our situation. A modern philosophy cannot develop without elucidating its roots in time and in a particular place. But even though we are subject to the conditions of our epoch, it is not from these conditions that we draw our philosophy, but now as at all times from the Comprehensive. We must not adjust our potentialities to the low level of our age, not subordinate ourselves to our epoch, but attempt, by elucidating the age, to arrive at the point where we can live out of our primal source.

Nor must we deify history. We need not accept the

godless maxim that history is the last judgment. It is no ultimate instance. Failure is no argument against the truth that is rooted in transcendence. By making history our own, we cast an anchor through history into eternity.

X

THE
INDEPENDENT PHILOSOPHER

THE INDEPENDENCE OF man is rejected by all totalitarianism, by the totalitarian religion which claims exclusive truth as well as by the totalitarian state which, melting down all humanity into material for its edifice of power, leaves no room for individuality and even controls leisure activities in accordance with an ideological line. Today independence seems to be silently disappearing beneath the inundation of all life by the typical, the habitual, the unquestioned commonplace.

But to philosophize is to fight for our inner independence, under all conditions. What is inner independence?

Since late antiquity the philosopher has been represented as an independent man. The portrait has certain salient features: This philosopher is independent, first because he is without needs, free from the world of possessions and the rule of passions, he is an ascetic; second, because he is without fear, for he has seen through the illusory terrors of the religions; third, because he takes no part in government and politics and lives without ties, in peaceful retirement, a citizen of the world. In any case this philosopher believes that he has attained to a position of absolute independence, a vantage point outside of things, in which he cannot be moved or shaken.

This philosopher has become an object of admiration but also of distrust. True, numerous philosophers of this type have disclosed rare independence through poverty, celibacy, aloofness from business and politics; they have manifested a happiness which did not spring from anything eternal but from awareness that life is a journey and from indifference to the blows of fate. But some of these figures also reveal egoism and ambition, pride and vanity, a coldness in human dealings and an ugly hostility to other philosophers. And dogmatism is common to all of them. Theirs is an impure independence which seems very much akin to an ununderstood and sometimes ridiculous dependence.

Nevertheless, side by side with biblical religion these philosophers do offer a historical source of possible independence. Acquaintance with them encourages our own striving for independence, perhaps precisely by showing us that man cannot sustain himself in isolation and detachment. This ostensible absolute freedom turns automatically into a new dependence, outwardly on the world, whose recognition is courted, inwardly on unclarified passions. The road of the philosophers of late antiquity offers us no promise. Although some were magnificent personalities, they created, in their fight for freedom, rigid figures and masks without background.

We see that independence turns into its opposite

if it is held to be absolute. And it is not easy to say in what sense we can strive for independence.

The concept of independence is almost hopelessly ambivalent. For example:

The philosopher, and the metaphysician in particular, sets up thought structures like games to which he remains superior because of his unlimited power over them. But this gives rise to the question: Is man master of his thoughts because he is godless and can carry on his creative game without reference to a foundation, arbitrarily, according to rules which he himself has devised, enchanted by its form, or conversely, because he is oriented toward God and thus remains superior to the discourse in which he must inevitably clothe absolute being, which can never fit the absolute, and hence needs to be readjusted ad infinitum?

Here the independence of the philosopher consists in his not succumbing to his ideas as dogmas but in making himself master over them. But mastery over one's ideas remains ambivalent—does it mean an arbitrary freedom from ties or does it imply ties in transcendence?

Another example: In order to gain our independence we seek an Archimedean point outside of the world. This is an authentic quest, but the question is: Is this Archimedean point an outsideness which makes man a kind of God in his total independence or is it the outside point where he truly meets God and experiences his only complete independence, which alone can make him independent in the world?

Because of this ambivalence, independence, instead of becoming a road to authentic selfhood in historic fulfilment, can easily be confused with irresponsibility, or the perpetual availability for something else. Then selfhood is lost, and all that remains is different roles played in different situations. This pseudo-independence, like all delusions, takes on countless forms. For example:

It can take the form of an aesthetic attitude toward all things, regardless of whether these things be men, animals, or stones. The resulting vision may have the force of a mythical perception, yet such a perception is "dead with waking eyes," since it does not carry the decision in which life is grounded; those who perceive things in this way may be prepared to commit themselves to the point of risking their lives but not to anchor themselves in the unconditional. Insensitive to contradictions and absurdities, avid for perceptions, they live amid the pressures of the age, striving to be affected as little as possible by those pressures, to carry on in the independence of their own will and experience, to live a life which responds outwardly to every pressure but retains an inner insensitivity, finding the summit of existence in the formulation of things seen, mistaking speech for being.

Those who cultivate this independence of irresponsibility shun self-awareness. The pleasure of vision becomes assimilated to passion for being. Being seems to reveal itself in this mythical thinking, which is a kind of speculative poetry.

But being does not reveal itself to the mere passion of vision. The most serious solitary vision, the most eloquent turns of phrase and striking images, in disregard of communication—all this dictatorial language of wisdom and prophecy is not enough.

Thus those who are deluded into supposing that they possess being as such often endeavour to make man forget himself. Man is dissolved in fictions of being and yet these fictions themselves always conceal a possible road back to man; hidden dissatisfaction may lead to the recovery of the authentic seriousness which becomes real only in existential presence and casts off the ruinous attitude of those who take life as it is and do what they please.

This irresponsible type of independence is also manifested in intellectual opportunism. An irresponsible playing with contradictions permits such a man to take any position he finds convenient. He is versed in all methods but adheres strictly to none. He espouses an unscientific attitude but makes scientific gestures. He is a Proteus, wriggling and changing, you cannot grasp hold of him, he actually says nothing but seems to be promising something extraordinary. He exerts an attraction by vague hints and whisperings which give men a sense of the mysterious. No authentic discussion with him is possible but only a talking back and forth about a wide variety of "interesting" things. Conversation with him can be no more than an aimless pouring forth of false emotion.

Irresponsible independence can take the form of indifference to a world that has grown intolerable.

What does death matter? It will come. What is there to be perturbed about?

We live in the joy of our vitality and the pain of its

ebbing away. A natural Yes permits us at all times to feel and to think according to circumstance. We are unpolemical. What is the good of taking sides? Love and tenderness are possible but they are at the mercy of time, of the ephemeral, of the transient as such. Nothing is unconditional.

We drift along, without desire to do or to be anything in particular. We do what is asked of us or what seems appropriate. Genuine emotion is absurd. We are helpful in our everyday dealings with men.

No horizon, no distance, neither past nor future sustain this life which expects nothing and lives only here and now.

The many forms of illusory independence to which we can succumb cast suspicion upon independence itself. This much is certain: in order to gain true independence we must not only elucidate these various forms of independence but achieve awareness of the limits of all independence.

Absolute independence is impossible. In thinking we are dependent on experience which must be given us, in living we are dependent on others with whom we stand in a relation of mutual aid. As selfhood we ate dependent on other selfhood, and it is only in communication that we and the others come truly to ourselves. There is no isolated freedom. Where there is freedom it struggles with unfreedom, and if unfreedom were fully overcome through the elimination of all resistances freedom itself would cease.

Accordingly, we are independent only when we are at the same time enmeshed in the world. I cannot achieve independence by abandoning the world. Indeed, independence in the world implies a particular attitude toward the world: to be in it and yet not in it, to be both inside it and outside it. This thought is shared by great thinkers of the most varying trends:

With regard to all experiences, pleasures, states of happiness and unhappiness, Aristippus says: I have, but I am not had; St. Paul tells his followers how to take part in earthly life: have as though you had not; the Bhagavad-Gita admonishes us to perform the task but not to strive after its fruits; Lao Tse counsels man to act through inaction.

These immortal sayings might be interpreted ad infinitum. Here we need only say that they all express inner independence. Our independence of the world is inseparable from a mode of dependence on the world.

A second limit to independence is that by itself alone it negates itself:

Independence has been negatively formulated as freedom from fear, as indifference to fortune, good or bad, as the imperturbability of the thinker as mere spectator, as immunity to emotions and impulses. But the self who achieves such independence is reduced to the abstract punctuality of the ego.

Independence does not derive its content from itself. It is not any innate gift, it is not vitality, race, the will to power, it is not self-creation.

Philosophical thought grows out of an independence in the world, an independence signifying an absolute attachment to the world through transcending of the world. A supposed independence without attachment becomes at once empty, that is, formal thinking, which is not present in its content, which does not participate in its idea, which is not grounded in existence. This independence becomes arbitrariness, particularly in negation. It costs nothing to question everything when there is no power to guide and bind the question.

The contrary is stated in Nietzsche's radical thesis: Only when there is no God does man become free. For if there is a God man does not grow, because he flows as it were continuously into God like an undammed brook, which gathers no force. But using the same figure we might say the reverse: Only with his eyes to God does man grow instead of seeping away undammed into the meaninglessness of life's mere happenings.

A third limit to our independence is the basic nature of man. As man we suffer from fundamental weaknesses from which we cannot free ourselves. With the first awakening of our consciousness we fall into error.

In the Bible this thought is expressed in mythical terms as the fall of man. In Hegel's philosophy man's alienation is magnificently elucidated. Kierkegaard speaks poignantly of the demonic in us, which drives us to despair and isolation. Sociology refers with less subtlety to the ideologies, psychology to the complexes which dominate us.

Can we master our inhibition and forgetfulness, our cloakings and concealings, our perversions, so as to attain to our authentic independence? St. Paul showed that we cannot be truly good. For without knowledge it is impossible to do good, and if I know that my action is good I sin by pride and certainty. Kant showed that we do good only under the tacit condition that our good action will not be too harmful to our happiness, and that this makes our good deed impure. This is a radical evil that we cannot overcome.

Our independence itself requires help. We can only do our best and hope that something within us—invisible to the world—will in some unfathomable way come to our aid and lift us out of our limitations. The only independence possible for us is dependence on transcendence.

I should like to give some intimation of how a measure of independence can be achieved in philosophical thought today:

Let us not pledge ourselves to any philosophical school or take formulable truth as such for the one and exclusive truth; let us be master of our thoughts;

let us not heap up philosophical possessions, but apprehend philosophical thought as movement and seek to deepen it;

let us battle for truth and humanity in unconditional communication;

let us acquire the power to learn from all the past by making it our own; let us listen to our contemporaries and remain open to all possibilities;

let each of us as an individual immerse himself in his own historicity, in his origin, in what he has done; let him possess himself of what he was, of what he has become, and of what has been given to him;

let us not cease to grow through our own historicity into the historicity of man as a whole and thus make ourselves into citizens of the world.

We lend little credence to a philosopher who is imperturbable, we do not believe in the calm of the Stoic, we do not even desire to be unmoved, for it is our humanity itself which drives us into passion and fear and causes us in tears and rejoicing to experience what is. Consequently only by rising from the chains that bind us to our emotions, not by destroying them, do we come to ourselves. Hence we must venture to be men and then do what we can to move forward to our true independence. Then we shall suffer without complaining, despair without succumbing; we shall be shaken but not overturned, for the inner independence that grows up in us will sustain us.

Philosophy is the school of this independence, it is not the possession of independence.

XI

THE PHILOSOPHICAL LIFE

IF OUR LIVES are not to be diffuse and meaningless, they must find their place in an order. In our daily affairs we must be sustained by a comprehensive principle, we must find meaning in an edifice of work, fulfilment, and sublime moments, and by repetition we must gain in depth. Then our lives, even in the performance of monotonous tasks, will be permeated by a mood arising from our conscious participation in a meaning. Then we shall be sustained by an awareness of the world and of ourselves, by the history of which we are a part, and, in our own lives, by memory and loyalty.

An order of this sort may come to the individual from the world in which he was born, from the church which shapes and animates the great steps from birth to death and the little steps of everyday life. He will then spontaneously fit his daily experience into that order. Not so in a crumbling world, which puts less and less faith in tradition, in a world which subsists only as outward order, without symbolism and transcendence, which leaves the soul empty and is not adequate to man, which, when it leaves him free, thrusts him back upon his own resources, in lust and boredom, fear and indifference. Here the individual can rely only in himself. By living philosophically he seeks to build up by his own strength what his world no longer gives him.

The desire to lead a philosophical life springs from the darkness in which the individual finds himself, from his sense of forlornness when he stares without love into the void, from his self-forgetfulness when he feels that he is being consumed by the busy-ness of the world, when he suddenly wakes up in terror and asks himself: What am I, what am I failing to do, what should I do?

That self-forgetfulness has been aggravated by the machine age. With its time clocks, its jobs, whether absorbing or purely mechanical, which less and less fulfil man as man, it may even lead man to feel that he is part of the machine, interchangeably shunted in here and there, and when left free, to feel that he is nothing and can do nothing with himself. And just as he begins to recover himself, the colossus of this world draws him back again into the all-consuming machinery of empty labour and empty leisure.

But man as such inclines to self-forgetfulness. He must snatch himself out of it if he is not to lose himself to the world, to habits, to thoughtless banalities, to the beaten track.

Philosophy is the decision to awaken our primal source, to find our way back to ourselves, and to help ourselves by inner action.

True, our first duty in life is to perform our practical tasks, to meet the demands of the day. But if we desire to lead a philosophical life we shall not content ourselves with practical tasks; we shall look upon the mere work in whose aims we immerse ourselves as in itself a road to self-forgetfulness, omission, and guilt. And to lead a philosophical life means also to take seriously our experience of men, of happiness and hurt, of success and failure, of the obscure and the confused. It means not to forget but to possess ourselves inwardly of our experience, not to let ourselves be distracted but to think problems through, not to take things for granted but to elucidate them.

There are two paths of philosophical life: the path of solitary meditation in all its ramifications and the path of communication with men, of mutual understanding through acting, speaking, and keeping silence together.

We men cannot do without our daily moments of profound reflection. In them we recapture our self-awareness, lest the presence of the primal source be lost entirely amid the inevitable distractions of daily life.

What the religions accomplish in prayer and worship has its philosophical analogy in explicit immersion, in inner communion with being itself. This can take place only in times and moments (regardless whether at the beginning or end of the day or in between) when we are not occupied in the world with worldly aims and yet are not left empty but are in contact with what is most essential.

Unlike religious contemplation, philosophical contemplation has no holy object, no sacred place, no fixed form. The order which we give to it does not become a rule, it remains potentiality in free motion.

This contemplation, unlike religious worship, demands solitude.

What is the possible content of such meditation?

First, self-reflection. I call to mind what I have done, thought, felt during the day. I ask myself wherein I have erred, wherein I have been dishonest with myself, wherein I have evaded my responsibilities, wherein I have been insincere; I also try to discern what good qualities I have displayed and seek ways in which to enhance them. I reflect on the degree of conscious control over my actions that I have exerted in the course of the day. I judge myself with regard to my particular conduct, not with regard to the whole man that I am, for that is inaccessible to me—I find principles in accordance with which I resolve to judge myself, perhaps I fix in my mind words that I plan to address to myself in anger, in despair, in boredom, and in other states in which the self is lost, magic words as it were, reminders (such as: observe moderation, think of the other, be patient, God is). I learn from the tradition that runs from the Pythagoreans through the Stoics and Christians to Kierkegaard and Nietzsche, with its injunction to self-reflection; I realize that such reflection can never be conclusive and that it is infinitely susceptible to error.

Second, transcending reflection. Guided by philosophical methods, I gain awareness of authentic being, of the godhead. I read the symbols of being with the help of literature and art. I gain understanding of them by philosophical scrutiny. I seek to ascertain that which is independent of time or that which is eternal in time, seek to touch upon the source of my freedom and through it upon being itself; I seek as it were to partake of creation.

Third, I reflect on what *should be done in the present*. Remembrance of my own life with men is the background against which I clarify my present task down to the details of this particular day, when in the inevitable intensity of practical thinking I lose my awareness of the Comprehensive meaning.

What I gain for myself alone in reflection would—if it were all—be as nothing gained.

What is not realised in communication is not yet, what is not ultimately grounded in it is without adequate foundation. The truth begins with two.

Consequently philosophy demands: seek constant communication, risk it without reserve, renounce the defiant self-assertion which forces itself upon you in ever new disguises, live in the hope that in your very renunciation you will in some incalculable way be given back to yourself.

Hence I must constantly draw myself into doubt, I must not grow secure, I must not fasten on to any ostensible light within myself, in the belief that it will illumine me reliably and judge me truly. Such an attitude toward the self is the most seductive form of inauthentic self-assertion.

If I meditate in these three forms—self-reflection, transcending meditation, contemplation of my task— and open myself to unlimited communication, an imponderable presence which can never be forced may come to me: the clarity of my love, the hidden and always uncertain imperative of the godhead, the revelation of being—perhaps bringing with it peace of mind amid life's constant turmoil, a trust in the foundation of things despite the most terrible catastrophes, unswerving resolve amid the vacillations of passion, a firm loyalty amid the momentary lures of this world.

If in my meditation I achieve awareness of the Comprehensive out of which I live and can live better, meditation will provide the dominant tone that carries me through the day in its countless activities, even while I am being swept along by the technical machine. For in these moments when I return home as it were to myself I acquire an underlying harmony which persists behind the moods and movements of the day, which sustains me and in all my derailment, confusion, emotional upheaval does not let me sink into the abyss. For these moments give to the present both memory and future, they give my life cohesion and continuity.

To philosophize is then at once to learn how to live and to know how to die. Because of the uncertainty of temporal existence life is always an experiment.

In this experiment the essential is that we dare to immerse ourselves in it, neither shunning nor closing our eyes to the extreme, and that we let unlimited integrity govern our vision, our questioning and our answering. And then let us go our way, without knowing the whole, without tangibly possessing the authentic, without letting false arguments or illusory experience provide us with a peephole, as it were, by which to look objectively and immediately out of the world into transcendence, without hearing any direct and unequivocal word of God, but reading the symbols of the polyvalent language of things and yet living with the certainty of transcendence.

Only transcendence can make this questionable life good, the world beautiful, and existence itself a fulfilment.

If to philosophize is to learn how to die, then we must learn how to die in order to lead a good life. To learn to live and to learn how to die are one and the same thing.

Meditation teaches us the *power of thought*.

Thought is the beginning of human existence. In accurate knowledge of objects I experience the power of the rational, as in the operations of mathematics, in the natural sciences, in technical planning. As my method grows purer, the logic of my syllogisms becomes more compelling, I gain greater insight into chains of causality, my experience becomes more reliable.

But philosophical thought begins at the limits of this rational knowledge. Rationality cannot help us in the essentials: it cannot help us to posit aims and ultimate ends, to know the highest good, to know God and human freedom; this inadequacy of the rational gives rise to a kind of thinking which, while working with the tools of the understanding, is more than understanding. Philosophy presses to the limits of rational knowledge and there takes fire.

He who believes that he understands everything is no longer engaged in philosophical thought. He who takes scientific insight for knowledge of being itself and as a whole has succumbed to scientific superstition.

He who has ceased to be astonished has ceased to question. He who acknowledges no mystery is no longer a seeker. Because he humbly acknowledges the limits of possible knowledge the philosopher remains open to the unknowable that is revealed at those limits.

Here cognition ceases, but not thought. By technically applying my knowledge I can act outwardly, but nonknowledge makes possible an inner action by which I transform myself. This is another and deeper kind of thought; it is not detached from being and oriented toward an object but is a process of my innermost self, in which thought and being become identical. Measured by outward, technical power, this thought of inner action is as nothing, it is no applied knowledge that can be possessed, it cannot be fashioned according to plan and purpose; it is an authentic illumination and growth into being.

The understanding (*ratio*) broadens our horizons; it fixates objects, reveals the tensions of the existent, and also permits what it cannot apprehend to stand forth in full force and clarity. The clarity of the understanding makes possible clarity at its limits, and arouses the authentic impulses which are thought and action, inward and outward act in one.

The philosopher is expected to live according to his doctrine. This maxim expresses poorly the thought that lies behind it. For the philosopher has no doctrine if by doctrine is meant a set of rules under which the particular cases of empirical existence might be subsumed, as things are subsumed under empirical species or men's acts under juridical norms. Philosophical ideas cannot be applied; they are a reality in

themselves, so that we may say: in the fulfilment of
these thoughts the man himself lives; or life is permeated with thought. That is why the philosopher
and the man are inseparable (while man can be considered apart from his scientific knowledge); and that
is why we cannot explore philosophical ideas in themselves but must at the same time gain awareness of the
philosophical humanity which conceived them.

Philosophical life is in constant peril of straying into
perversions in justification of which philosophical
propositions are invoked. The formulae which elucidate existence are distorted by the vital will:

Peace of mind is confused with passivity, confidence
with an illusory faith in the harmony of all things,
knowing how to die is mistaken for flight from the
world, reason for total indifference. The best is
perverted to the worst.

The will to communication is perverted into self-
contradictory attitudes: we wish to be undisturbed,
yet demand absolute self-certainty in self-illumination.
We wish to be excused because of our nerves and yet
ask to be recognized as free. We are cautious and taci-
turn, and secretly on our guard even while professing
unreserved readiness for communication. We think of
ourselves while we are supposedly speaking of the
idea.

The philosopher who strives to understand and overcome these perversions in himself knows his uncertainty; he is always on the lookout for criticism, he
seeks opposition and wishes to be called to question;
he desires to listen, not in order to submit but in order

to be spurred onward in self-illumination. Where there is open and unreserved communication this philosopher finds truth and unsought-for confirmation in harmony with the other.

Philosophy must even leave the possibility of full communication in uncertainty, though it lives by faith in communication and stakes everything on communication. We can believe in it but not know it. To believe that we possess it is to have lost it.

For there are terrible limits which philosophical thought has never recognized as definitive; limits at which we forget or at which we accept and recognize notions which we have not thoroughly elucidated. Alas, we talk so much when what really matters can be stated so simply, not in a universal proposition to be sure, but in a concrete symbol.

In the face of perversions, involvements, and confusions, modern man calls the doctor. And indeed there are diseases and neuroses which strongly effect our mental condition. The attempt to diagnose them, to understand them, to treat them is perfectly realistic. There is no reason to shun the human agency of the physician, when through critical experience he has gained real knowledge and ability. But certain modern developments in the field of psychotherapy are no longer grounded in medical science but in philosophy, so that like any other philosophical effort they demand to be examined from the point of view of ethics and metaphysics.

The goal of a philosophical life cannot be formulated as a state of being, which is attainable and once

attained, perfect. Our states of being are only manifestations of existential striving or failure. It lies in our very
nature to be on-the-way. We strive to cut across
time. That is possible only in polarities:

Only when we exist entirely in this time of our
historicity can we experience something of the eternal
present.

Only as determinate men, each in his specificity, can
we experience humanity as such.

Only when we experience our own age as our
Comprehensive reality can we apprehend this age as
part of the unity of history, and this unity of history as
part of eternity.

In our ascending journey the primal source grows
clearer for us behind our empirical states, but there is
constant danger that it will return to obscurity.

The ascent of philosophical life is the ascent of the
individual man. He must accomplish it as an individual
in communication and cannot shift responsibility to
others.

We achieve this ascent in the historically concrete,
elective acts of our life, not by electing any so-called
weltanschauung laid down in propositions.

And now, in conclusion, let us venture a metaphor
that may characterize the situation of philosophy in
the temporal world:

Having oriented himself on secure dry land—
through realistic observation, through the special
sciences, through logic and methodology—the
philosopher, at the limits of this land, explores the
world of ideas over tranquil paths. And now like a
butterfly he flutters over the ocean shore, darting out

over the water; he spies a ship in which he would like to go on a voyage of discovery, to seek out the one thing which as transcendence is present in his existence. He peers after the ship—the method of philosophical thought and philosophical life—the ship which he sees and yet can never fully reach; and he struggles to reach it, sometimes strangely staggering and reeling.

We are creatures of this sort, and we are lost if we relinquish our orientation to the dry land. But we are not content to remain there. That is why our flutterings are so uncertain and perhaps so absurd to those who sit secure and content on dry land, and are intelligible only to those who have been seized by the same unrest. For them the world is a point of departure for that flight upon which everything depends, which each man must venture on his own though in common with other men, and which can never become the object of any doctrine.

XII

THE HISTORY OF PHILOSOPHY

PHILOSOPHY IS AS old as religion and older than the churches. In the stature and purity of its champions and in the integrity of its spirit it has usually, though not always, been on a level with the world of the church, whose rights it recognizes in its specific sphere. But without sociological form of its own it has been helpless in its confrontation with the church. It has enjoyed the accidental protection of powers in the world, including the church. It requires favourable sociological situations in order to reveal itself in objective works. Its authentic reality is open to every man at all times, and it is in some form omnipresent wherever there are men.

The churches are for all, philosophy for individuals. The churches are visible organizations, wielding power over masses of men in the world. Philosophy is an expression of a realm of minds linked with one another through all peoples and ages; it is represented by no institution which excludes or welcomes.

As long as the churches have ties with the Eternal, their outward power exploits the innermost energies. As they draw the Eternal into the service of their power in the world, this power, like every other power in the world, grows sinister and evil.

As long as philosophy remains in contact with eternal truth it inspires without violence, it brings order to the soul, from its innermost source. But when it places its truth in the service of temporal powers it beguiles men to delude themselves for the benefit of their practical concerns, it leads to anarchy of the soul. And when it aspires to be no more than a science it becomes an empty game, which is neither science nor philosophy.

Independent philosophy comes to no man of itself. No one is born into it. It must always be acquired anew. It can be apprehended only by him who perceives it out of his own source. The first ever-so-fleeting perception of it can fire a man with enthusiasm. The enthusiasm for philosophy is followed by the study of philosophy.

The study of philosophy takes three forms: practical study, in the inward action of each day; specialized study, in the learning of the contents, the study of the sciences, of the categories, methods and systems; historical study, by which we make the philosophical tradition our own. The reality that speaks to him from the history of philosophy is for the philosopher what authority is for the churchman.

If the history of philosophy is to further our own philosophical efforts, it must be understood in the broadest possible sense.

The variety of philosophical manifestations is extraordinary. The Upanishads were conceived in the Indian villages and forests, apart from the world, by hermits or small groups of teachers and students; Kautilya was a minister who founded an empire, Confucius a teacher who wished to restore education and true political reality to his people; Plato was an

aristocrat who felt that he could not engage in the
political activity befitting his rank because of its
moral degeneration: Bruno, Descartes, Spinoza
were solitary thinkers, without any institution behind
them, seeking the truth for its own sake; Anselm was
the founder of an ecclesiastical aristocracy; Thomas a
servant of the church; Nicholas of Cusa a cardinal
whose ecclesiastical and philosophical life were one;
Machiavelli an unsuccessful statesman; Kant, Hegel,
Schelling, professors who developed their philosophies
in connection with their teaching.

We must rid ourselves of the idea that philosophical
activity as such is the affair of professors. It would
seem to be the affair of man, under all conditions and
circumstances, of the slave as of the ruler. We understand the historical manifestation of the truth only if we
examine it in conjunction with the world in which it
arose and the destinies of the men who conceived it.
If these manifestations are remote and alien to us, this
in itself is illuminating. We must seek the philosophical
idea and the thinker in their physical reality. The
truth does not hover all alone in the air of abstraction.

The history of philosophy comes alive for us when,
by thorough study of a work and of the world in which
it was produced, we participate as it were in that work.

After that we seek perspectives which will accord
us a view of the history of philosophy as a whole, in
schemas which, though questionable, serve as guides
by which to orient ourselves in so vast a region.

The whole of the history of philosophy throughout
two and a half millennia is like a single vast moment

in the growing self-awareness of man. This moment may be looked upon as a never-ending discussion, disclosing clashes of forces, questions that seem insoluble, sublime works and regressions, profound truth and a turmoil of error.

In our study of the history of philosophy we seek a framework in which to situate philosophical ideas. Only through the history of philosophy as a whole can we learn how philosophy developed in relation to the most diverse social and political conditions and personal situations.

Philosophy developed independently in China, India, and the West. Despite occasional intercommunication, these three worlds were so sharply separate down to the time of Christ's birth that each one must in the main be studied in its own terms. After this date the strongest influence was that of Indian Buddhism on China, comparable to that of Christianity on the Western world.

In the three worlds the development follows a similar curve. After a preliminary history which it is difficult to clarify, the fundamental ideas rose everywhere in the axial age (800–200 B.C.). After this there was a period of dissolution in the course of which the great religions of redemption were consolidated; there were recurrent periods of renewal; there were all-embracing systems (Scholasticism) and logical speculations of sublime metaphysical import, carried to the utmost extreme.

What was the specific Western character of this synchronistic development? First it consisted in a greater dynamism, bringing with it constant crises and developments; second, in the greater diversity of languages and peoples manifesting the ideas; and third, in the unique development of Western science.

Western philosophy falls historically into four periods:

First: *Greek philosophy* travelled the path from myth to logos, created the basic Western concepts, the categories and fundamental conceptions of being as a whole, of the world and man. For us it remains the archetype of simplicity; in making it our own we preserve our clarity.

Second: *Christian-medieval philosophy* travelled the path from biblical religion to its conceptual understanding, from revelation to theology. It was more than a conservative pedagogic Scholasticism. Creative thinkers, chief among them St. Paul, St. Augustine, Martin Luther, disclosed a world which in its source was religious and philosophical in one. For us it remains to preserve alive in our minds the secret of Christianity as manifested in this wide realm of thought.

Third: *Modern European philosophy* arose hand in hand with modern natural science and man's new personal rejection of all authority. Kepler and Galileo on the one hand, Bruno and Spinoza on the other represent the new roads. For us it remains to preserve the true meaning of science as they apprehended it—although it was also perverted from the very outset—and of spiritual freedom.

Fourth: *The philosophy of German idealism.* From Lessing and Kant to Hegel and Schelling we have a series of thinkers who perhaps excel all previous

Western thought in contemplative depth. Without the background of a great political and social reality, working in privacy and seclusion, filled with the whole of history and the cosmos, rich in the speculative art of thought and in visions of human contents, though they had no real world, they erected great works which contained a world. For us it remains to gain from them as much as possible of the depth and scope which otherwise would be lost.

Up to the seventeenth century and even longer all Western thought was guided by the ancients, the Bible, St. Augustine. Since the eighteenth century this has gradually ceased to be so. Since then thinkers have believed that they could build without history, upon their own reason alone. While traditional thought vanished as an effective force, there developed a learned approach to the history of philosophy, but it was limited to a few men. Today scholarly editions and reference works have made the tradition more easily accessible than ever before.

In the twentieth century there has been an accelerated tendency to forget the millennial foundations in favour of diffuse technical knowledge and skills, of scientific superstition, illusory worldly aims, and intellectual passivity.

By the middle of the nineteenth century men began to feel that an end had come and to ask themselves whether philosophy was still possible. The continuity of modern philosophy in the Western countries, the professorial philosophy of Germany, cultivating a historic sense of the great tradition, could not hide the fact that a form of philosophical thought which had endured for a thousand years was drawing to a close.

The representative philosophers of the epoch are Kierkegaard and Nietzsche, thinkers of a type which had formerly not existed, clearly related to the crisis of this age; and Marx who, intellectually a world apart from them, excelled all modern philosophers in mass influence.

An extreme thinking became possible, which questioned everything in order to penetrate to the profoundest source, which shook off all encumbrances in order to free the vision for an insight into existence, the unconditional, and actuality, in a world that had been radically transformed by the technological age.

We draw up schemas of this sort in envisaging the history of philosophy as a whole. They are superficial. In our search for deeper meanings we may touch on such questions as these:

First: *Is there a unity in the history of philosophy?* This unity is not fact but idea. We seek it but attain only to particular unities.

Certain problems (such as the relation between body and soul) come into focus at various times, but the historical factors coincide only partially with a logical construction of the ideas. Progressions of systems can be shown; it can be shown, for example, how, as Hegel saw it, German philosophy and ultimately all philosophy culminated in his own system. But constructions of this sort do violence to the facts, they fail to take into account those elements in earlier philosophical thought which are fatal to Hegelian thinking and are hence ignored by Hegel;

the philosophers who erect them tend to neglect the very essence of other men's thinking. No construction of the history of philosophy as a logically coherent series of positions coincides with historical fact.

Any unified construction we can give to the history of philosophy is vitiated by the genius of the individual philosopher. Despite all demonstrable ties and influences, greatness remains an incomparable miracle, quite apart from the development that is accessible to our understanding.

The idea of a unity in the history of philosophy may apply to that perennial philosophy which is internally one, which creates its historical organs and structures, its garments and tools, but is not identical with them.

Second: *The beginning and its significance.* The beginning is the first appearance of an idea, at some moment in time. The source is the fundamental truth that is always present.

From misunderstandings and perversions of thought we must at all times return to the source. Instead of seeking this source by following the guidance of meaningful, transmitted texts, some thinkers fall into the error of seeking it in temporal beginnings: e.g., in the first pre-Socratic philosophers, in early Christianity, in early Buddhism. The journey to the source which is always necessary assumes the false form of a search for the beginnings.

It is true that those beginnings which are still attainable exert a powerful spell. But an absolute beginning cannot be found. What passes in our tradition for a beginning is a relative beginning and was itself the product of earlier development.

Hence it is a fundamental principle of historical study that in examining transmitted texts we restrict ourselves to their real content. Only through a historical attitude can we deepen our insight into what has been preserved. There is nothing to be gained by reconstituting what has been lost, by reconstructing earlier phases, by filling in gaps.

Third: *Can we speak of development and progress in philosophy?* We can observe certain lines of development, for example: from Socrates to Plato and Aristotle, from Kant to Hegel, from Locke to Hume. But even such sequences are false if we take them to mean that the later thinker preserved and transcended the truth of his predecessor. Even where generations are thus visibly linked, the new is not encompassed in what went before. The successor often relinquishes the essence of the earlier thought, sometimes he no longer even understands it.

There are worlds of intellectual exchange which endure for a time, to which the individual thinker contributes his word, as for example, Greek philosophy, Scholastic philosophy, the "German philosophical movement" from 1760 to 1840. These are epochs of living communion in original thought. There are other epochs in which philosophy endures as pedagogy, others in which it almost seems to have vanished.

The total view of the history of philosophy as a progressive development is misleading. The history of philosophy resembles the history of art in that its supreme works are irreplaceable and unique. It resembles the history of science in that its tools—

categories and methods—have multiplied and are used with greater understanding. It resembles the history of religion in that it constitutes a succession of original acts of faith, though here expressed in terms of ideas.

The history of philosophy also has its creative epochs. But philosophy is at all times an essential preoccupation of man. It differs from other branches of spiritual endeavour in that a philosopher of the first order can suddenly appear in a supposed period of decadence. Plotinus in the third century, Scotus Erigena in the ninth century are isolated figures, unique summits. Their terminology fits into the tradition, possibly all their ideas derive from it, and yet as a whole they contribute a new fundamental pattern of thought.

Hence the very nature of philosophy forbids us to say that it is at an end. Philosophy endures in every catastrophe, in the thoughts of a few men, and in the isolated works which somehow appear in ages that are otherwise spiritually barren. Philosophy like religion exists at all times.

Another reason why development is a meaningless concept for the history of philosophy is that every great philosophy is complete and whole in itself, living by its own right, without reference to any broader historical truth. Science progresses step by step. But philosophy by its very nature must achieve wholeness in each individual man. Hence it is incongruous to speak of this or that philosopher as a mere milestone or precursor.

Fourth: *Can philosophers be classified by order of rank?*

141

Certain thinkers and epochs make it plain that the history of philosophy has its gradations. It is no level field in which all works and thinkers stand on an equal footing. There are heights of vision to which only a few have attained. And there are great men, suns amid the hosts of stars. But this does not mean that we can set up a definitive hierarchy which would carry conviction for everyone.

It is a far remove from the opinions held generally in a given epoch to the content of the philosophical works created in that epoch. That which the understanding of all men looks upon as self-evident, hence requiring no interpretation, can be expressed in the form of philosophy just as well as the great philosophic ideas that are susceptible of endless interpretation. A tranquil, limited vision and contentment with the world thus seen; the yearning for the unknown; and questioning at the limits—all these are philosophy.

We have spoken of an analogy between the history of philosophy and the authority of religious tradition. True, philosophy has no canonical books such as those possessed by the religions, no authority which need simply be followed, no definitive truth which simply exists. But the historical tradition of philosophy as a whole, this deposit of inexhaustible truth, shows us the roads to our present philosophical endeavour. The tradition is the profound truth of past thought, toward which we look with never-ending expectancy; it is something unfathomable in the few great works; it is the reality of the great thinkers, received with reverence.

The tradition is an authority that cannot be obeyed with certainty. It is incumbent upon us to come to ourselves through it by our own experience, to find our own source in its source.

Only in the seriousness of present philosophical thinking can we gain contact with eternal philosophy in its historical manifestation. It is through the historical manifestation that we gain the profound ties that can unite us in a common present.

Thus historical research is conducted on various levels. In his approach to the texts the conscientious student of philosophy knows on which plane he is moving. He must gain intelligent mastery of the "facts." But the end and summit of historical study lies in the moments of communion in the source. It is then that the light dawns which gives meaning and unity to all factual research. Without this centre, this philosophical source, the history of philosophy would be a mere record of fallacies and curiosities.

Once it has awakened me, history becomes the mirror of what is my own: in its image I see what I myself think.

The history of philosophy—a space in which I think and breathe—reveals in inimitable perfection prototypes for my own searching. By its attempts, its successes and failures, philosophy raises the question. It encourages me through the example of those men who have unswervingly followed its arduous path.

To take a past philosophy as our own is no more possible than to produce an old work of art for a second time. At best we can produce a deceptive copy. We have no text, like pious Bible readers, in which we may hope to find absolute truth. We love the old texts as we love old works of art, our hearts go out to them, we immerse ourselves in their truth, but there remains in them something remote and unattainable, unfathomable, though it is something with which we always live, something which starts us on the way to our present philosophizing.

For philosophy is essentially concerned with the present. We have only one reality, and that is here and now. What we miss by our evasions will never return, but if we squander ourselves, then too we lose being. Each day is precious: a moment can be everything.

We are remiss in our task if we lose ourselves in the past or future. Only through present reality can we gain access to the timeless; only in apprehending time can we attain to that sphere where all time is extinguished.

APPENDICES

PHILOSOPHY AND SCIENCE*

PHILOSOPHY HAS FROM its very beginnings looked upon itself as science, indeed as science par excellence. To achieve the highest and most certain knowledge is the goal that has always animated its devotees.

How its scientific character came to be questioned can be understood only in the light of the development of the specifically modern sciences. These sciences made their greatest strides in the nineteenth century, largely outside philosophy, often in opposition to philosophy, and finally in an atmosphere of indifference to it. If philosophy was still expected to be a science, it was in a different sense than before; it was now expected to be a science in the same sense as those modern sciences that convince by virtue of their accomplishments. If it were unable to do so, it was argued, it had become pointless and might just as well die out.

Some decades ago the opinion was widespread that philosophy had had its place up to the moment when all the sciences had become independent of it, the original universal science. Now that all possible fields of research have been marked off, the days of philosophy are over. Now that we know how science obtains its universal validity, it has become evident that philosophy cannot stand up against judgment by these criteria. It deals in empty ideas because it sets up

* Reprinted by permission of the *Partisan Review*.

undemonstrable hypotheses, it disregards experience, it seduces by illusions, it takes possession of energies needed for genuine investigation and squanders them in empty talk about the whole.

This was the picture of philosophy as seen against science conceived as methodical, cogent, universally valid insight. Under such circumstances could any philosophy legitimately claim to be scientific? To this situation philosophy reacted in two ways:

1) The attack was regarded as justified. Philosophers withdrew to limited tasks. If philosophy is at an end because the sciences have taken over all its subject matter, there remains nevertheless the knowledge of its history, first as a factor in the history of the sciences themselves, then as a phenomenon in the history of thought, the history of the errors, the anticipated insights, the process of liberation by which philosophy has made itself superfluous. Finally, the history of philosophy must preserve the knowledge of the philosophical texts, if only for their aesthetic interest. Although these texts do not make any serious contribution to scientific truth, they are nevertheless worth reading for the sake of their style and the intellectual attitude they reflect.

Others paid tribute to the modern scientific trend by rejecting all previous philosophy and striving to give philosophy an exact scientific foundation. They seized upon questions which, they claimed, were reserved for philosophy because they concern all the sciences; namely, logic, epistemology, phenomenology. In an effort to refurbish its reputation, philosophy became a servile imitator, a handmaiden to the sciences. It proceeded to establish in theory the validity of scientific knowledge, which was not questioned anyhow. But in the field of logic it developed a specialized science which because of the universality of its purpose, i.e., to define the form of all true thinking, to provide a *mathesis universalis*, seemed capable of replacing all previous philosophy. Today many thinkers regard symbolic logic as the whole of philosophy.

This first reaction seems today to have given rise to the view that philosophy is a science among other sciences, a discipline among other disciplines. And like the others, it is carried on by specialists. It has its narrow circle of experts, its congresses, and its learned periodicals.

2) In opposition to this infatuation with science there has been a second reaction. Philosophy attempted to save itself from destruction by dropping its claim to scientific knowledge. Philosophy—according to this view—is not a science at all. It is based on feeling and intuition, on imagination and genius. It is conceptual magic, not knowledge. It is *élan vital* or resolute acceptance of death. Indeed, some went further and said: It does not behoove philosophy to concern itself with science since it is aware that all scientific truth is questionable. The modern sciences are altogether in error, witness the ruinous consequences for the soul and for life in general of the rational attitude. Philosophy itself is not a science, and for that very reason its element is authentic truth.

Both reactions—submission to science and rejection of science conceived as cogent, methodical, and universally valid knowledge—seem to spell the end of philosophy. Whether it is the slave of science or whether it denies all science, it has in either case ceased to be philosophy.

The seeming triumph of the sciences over philosophy has for some decades created a situation in which philosophers go back to various sources in search of true philosophy. If such a thing is found, the question of the relation between philosophy and science will be answered, both in a theoretical and in a concrete sense. It is a practical question of the utmost urgency.

We shall appreciate the full weight of this problem if we consider its historical origin. It developed from three complexly intertwined factors. These are a) the spirit of modern science; b) the ancient and ever recurrent attempt to achieve universal philosophical knowledge; c) the philosophical concept of truth, as it was first and for all time elucidated in Plato.

Ad a) The modern sciences, developed only in the last few centuries, have brought into the world a new scientific attitude which existed neither in Asia nor in antiquity nor in the Middle Ages.

Even the Greeks, to be sure, conceived of science as methodical, cogently certain, and universally valid knowledge. But the modern sciences not only have brought out these basic attributes of science with greater purity (a task which has not yet been completed), they have also given new form and new foundation to the purpose, scope, and unity of their fields of inquiry. I shall indicate certain of their fundamental characteristics:

1) To modern science *nothing is indifferent*. In its eyes every fact, even the smallest and ugliest, the most distant and most alien, is a legitimate object of inquiry for the very reason that it exists. Science has become truly universal. There is nothing that can evade it. Nothing must be hidden or passed over in silence; nothing must remain a mystery.

2) Modern science is by definition unfinished, because it progresses toward the infinite, whereas ancient science in every one of its forms presented itself as finished; its actual development was in every case short lived, and it never set its own development as its conscious goal. Modern scientists have understood that an all-embracing world-system, which deduces everything that exists from one or a few principles, is impossible. A world-system has other sources and can only claim universal validity if scientific critique is relaxed and particulars are mistaken for absolutes. Such unprecedented systematizations as those achieved by modern physics cover only one aspect of reality. Through them reality as a whole has become more split up and deprived of foundations than it ever before seemed to the human mind. Hence the incompleteness of the modern world as compared to the Greek cosmos.

3) The ancient sciences remained *scattered*, unrelated to one another. They did not aim at constituting an all-embracing body of specific knowledge, whereas the modern sciences strive to be integrated into a universal frame of reference. Though a true world-system is no longer possible for them, a cosmos of the sciences is still conceivable. Our sense of the inadequacy of each

special branch of knowledge demands that each science be connected with knowledge as a whole.

4) The modern sciences attach little value to the *possibilities* of thought; they recognize the idea only in definite and concrete knowledge, after it has proved its worth as an instrument of discovery and been subjected to infinite modifications in the process of investigation. True, there is a certain similarity between ancient and modern atomic theory, in so far as the general pattern is concerned. But the ancient theory was merely an intrinsically finished interpretation of possibilities, based on plausible explanations of available experience, while the modern theory, in constant association with experience, undergoes perpetual change by confirmation and disproof and is itself an implement of investigation.

5) Today a scientific attitude has become possible, an attitude of inquiry toward all phenomena; today the scientist can know certain things clearly and definitely, he can distinguish between what he knows and what he does not know; and he has amassed an unprecedented abundance of knowledge (how very little the Greek physician or the Greek technician knew by comparison!). The moral imperative of modern science is to search for reliable knowledge on the basis of unprejudiced inquiry and critique, without any preconceived ideas. When we enter into its sphere, we have the sensation of breathing clean air, of leaving behind us all vague talk, all plausible opinions, all stubborn prejudice and blind faith.

Ad b) Modern science shares the age-old striving for total philosophical knowledge. Philosophy had from the first set itself up as the science that knows the whole—not as infinitely progressing, factual knowledge but as self-contained doctrine. Now modern philosophy since Descartes has identified itself with modern science but in such a way that it still retained the philosophical concept of a total knowledge. It can be shown, however, that for this very reason Descartes did not understand modern science, the investigations of Galileo for example, and that his own work had in spirit little to do with modern science, although as a creative mathematician he helped to advance this science. The ensuing philosophers, even to a certain extent Kant, were still caught in this totalist conception of science. Hegel once again believed that he was achieving the construction of an authentic total science and that he possessed all the sciences in his cosmos of the mind.

This identification of modern science and modern philosophy with their old aspiration to total knowledge was catastrophic for both of them. The modern sciences which, by a self-deception common to all of them, looked on those great philosophies of the seventeenth century and on some later philosophies as pillars of their own edifice were tainted by their aspirations to absolute knowledge. Modern philosophy has done its greatest work only "in spite of" all this, or one might say, by a constant misunderstanding.

Ad c) Neither the modern concept of science nor science in the sense of a total philosophical system coincides with the strictly philosophical conception of science which Plato formulated in a way that has never been surpassed. How far removed is the truth, the knowledge of which Plato interprets in his parable of the cave and touches on in his dialectic, this truth that applies to being and to that which is above all being— how fundamentally different it is from the truth of the sciences, which move only amid the manifestations of being without ever attaining to being itself, and how different from the truth of the dogmatic system which holds itself to be in possession of the whole of being. What a distance between the truth which can nowhere be set down in writing but which, according to Plato's seventh epistle, though it can only be attained by thought, is kindled in a favourable moment of communication among men of understanding, and the truth which is written, universally cogent and intelligible, distinct and available to all thinking creatures!

Three so different conceptions of scientific knowledge—the first patterned on the method of modern science, the second derived from the idea of a total philosophical system, and the third related to faith in a truth which is directly apprehended by the intellect (Plato's truth being an example)—all contribute to the present confusion. An example:

Its inquiries and investigations in the economic field have made Marxism an important force in scientific development. But this it shares with many other trends, and its scientific contribution does not account for its influence. Marxism also represents a philosophical thesis regarding the dialectical course of history as a total process which it purports to understand. Thus it constitutes a philosophical doctrine but one with a claim to universal scientific validity. It has the same epistemological basis as Hegel's philosophy, whose dialectical method remains its implement. The difference is only that for Hegel the core of the historical process lies in what he calls the "idea," while for Marx it lies in the mode of production of man who, unlike the animals, obtains his sustenance through systematic labour. Both Hegel and Marx derive all phenomena from what they regard as the core. Marx therefore rightly claims to have stood Hegel on his head; that however is only in content, for he did not depart from Hegel's method of constructing reality by the dialectic of the concept.

Now this identification of economic knowledge, which is gained by scientific method, hence inductively, and which by its very nature is subject to constant modifications, with the dialectical knowledge of the total process, which passes for essentially definitive knowledge, is the source of the fallacy committed by Hegel and in a different form by the type of modern philosophy that began with Descartes and was repeated by Marx. Marx's absolute, exclusive claim therefore originates in a conception of philosophy as total, systematic knowledge; but at the same time, his doctrine is presented as a result of modern science, from which it does not at all follow.

In addition to the conceptions patterned on modern science and total philosophy, there operates in Marxism also a third conception, reflecting the lofty idea of an absolute truth that fulfils man's will and aspirations, analogous to the Platonic idea of truth, although entirely different in character. Marxism conceives of itself as the true consciousness of the classless man.

This quasi-religious postulate is the source of a new kind of fanaticism which invokes not faith but modern science, which charges its opponents with stupidity, malice, or inability to overcome class prejudice and contrasts these with its own universal human truth that is free from class bondage and hence absolute.

Similar intellectual tendencies, which uncritically hypostatize a field of investigation that is meaningful within its limits into a total science and infuse it with a religious attitude, have been manifested in the domains of racial theory and psychoanalysis and in many other fields.

The false confusion of heterogeneous elements produces here, on a large scale, results that are so familiar on a small scale in everyday life—an attitude of never being at a loss for an answer, satisfaction with mere plausibility, stubbornly uncritical statements and affirmations, inability to explore in a genuine sense, to listen, analyse, test, and reflect on principles.

The infuriating part of it is that science is invoked to defend something that runs directly counter to the scientific spirit. For science leads us to the understanding of the principles, limitations, and meaning of our knowledge. It teaches us to know, in full consciousness of the methods by which each stage of knowledge is achieved. It produces a certainty whose relativity, i.e., dependence on presuppositions and methods of investigation, is its crucial characteristic.

Thus we are today confronted with an ambivalent concept of science. Genuine science can, as has always been the case, appear to be occult; it is in the nature of a public secret. It is public because it is accessible to everyone; it is a secret because it is far from being truly understood by everyone. All the more brightly shines the genuine, unswerving, never-failing scientific attitude, whose very critical awareness of its limits leaves room for every other source of truth in man.

In addition there is a wonderful virtue in science itself. In the course of scientific development only what is truly known is permanently preserved, the rest is eliminated through critique. So long as free discussion prevails, a body of knowledge forms that is more than the men who are its vehicle, a body of knowledge that no individual can encompass in all its scope.

At a time when confusion prevails regarding the meaning of science, three tasks are imperative, corresponding to the three tendencies discussed above.

First, the idea that total philosophical knowledge is scientific knowledge must be exposed as false. The sciences themselves critically explode this false total knowledge. It is here that the opposition to philosophy has its root, and in this respect contempt of it is justifiable.

Second, the sciences must be made pure. This can be accomplished through constant struggle and awareness in the course of our scientific activity itself. By and large, the need for basic clarity concerning science and its limits is readily admitted even by those who sin against such clarity in practice. But the essential is to achieve this purity within the specific sciences. This must be done largely through the critical work of the scientists themselves. But the philosopher who wishes to test the truth-meaning of scientific knowledge, to auscultate it, so to speak, must participate in the actual work of these scientists.

Third, a pure philosophy must be worked out in the new conditions that have been created by the modern sciences. This is indispensable for the sake of the sciences themselves. For philosophy is always alive in the sciences and so inseparable from them that the purity of both can be achieved only jointly. The rejection of philosophy usually leads to the unwitting development of a bad philosophy. The concrete work of the scientist is guided by his conscious or unconscious philosophy, and this philosophy cannot be the object of scientific method.

For example: It is impossible to prove scientifically that there should be such a thing as science. Or: The choice of an object of science that is made from among an infinite number of existing objects on the basis of this object itself is a choice that cannot be justified scientifically. Or: The ideas that guide us are tested in the systematic process of investigation, but they themselves do not become an object of direct investigation.

Science left to itself as mere science becomes homeless. The intellect is a whore, said Nicholas of Cusa, for it can prostitute itself to anything. Science is a whore, said Lenin, for it sells itself to any class interest. For Nicholas of Cusa it is Reason, and ultimately the knowledge of God, that gives meaning, certainty, and truth to intellectual knowledge; for Lenin, it is the classless society that promotes pure science. Be that as it may, awareness of all this is the business of philosophical reflection. Philosophy is inherent in the actual sciences themselves; it is their inner meaning that provides the scientist with sustenance and guides his methodical work. He who consolidates this guidance through reflection and becomes conscious of it has reached the stage of explicit philosophizing. If this guidance fails, science falls into gratuitous convention, meaningless correctness, aimless busy-ness, and spineless servitude.

A pure science requires a pure philosophy.

But how can philosophy be pure? Has it not always striven to be science? Our answer is: It is "science" but science of such a sort that in the sense of modern scientific inquiry it is both less and more than science.

Philosophy can be called science in so far as it presupposes the sciences. There is no tenable philosophy outside the sciences. Although conscious of its distinct character, philosophy is inseparable from science. It refuses to transgress against universally binding insight. Anyone who philosophizes must be familiar with scientific method.

Any philosopher who is not trained in a scientific discipline and who fails to keep his scientific interests constantly alive will inevitably bungle and stumble and mistake uncritical rough drafts for definitive knowledge. Unless an idea is submitted to the coldly dispassionate test of scientific inquiry, it is rapidly consumed in the fire of emotions and passions, or else it withers into a dry and narrow fanaticism.

Moreover, anyone who philosophizes strives for scientific knowledge, for it is the only way to genuine nonknowledge, it is as though the most magnificent insights could be achieved only through man's quest for the limit at which cognition runs aground, not seemingly and temporarily but genuinely and definitively, not with a sense of loss and despair but with a sense of genuine internal evidence. Only definitive knowledge can make definitive nonknowledge possible; it alone can achieve the authentic failure which opens up a vista, not merely upon the discoverable existent but upon being itself.

In accomplishing the great task of dispelling all magical conceptions, modern science enters upon the path that leads to the intuition of the true depth, the authentic mystery, which becomes present only through the most resolute knowledge in the consummation of nonknowledge.

Consequently philosophy turns against those who despise the sciences, against the sham prophets who deprecate scientific inquiry, who mistake the errors of science for science itself, and who would even hold science, "modern science," responsible for the evils and the inhumanity of our era.

Rejecting superstitious belief in science as well as contempt of science, philosophy grants its unconditional recognition to modern science. In its eyes science is a marvellous thing which can be relied upon more than anything else, the most significant achievement of man in his history, an achievement that is the source of great dangers but of even greater opportunities and that from now on must be regarded as a prerequisite of all human dignity. Without science, the philosopher knows, his own pursuits eventuate in nothing.

These pursuits can continue to be called scientific because philosophy proceeds methodically and because it is conscious of its methods. But these methods differ from those of science in that they have no object of inquiry. Any specific object is the object of a particular science. Were I to say that the object of philosophy is the whole, the world, being, philosophical critique would answer that such terms do not denote genuine objects. The methods of philosophy are methods of transcending the object. To philosophize is to transcend. But since our thinking is inseparable from objects, the history of philosophy is an account of how the progress of human thought has succeeded in transcending the objects of philosophy. These objects, the great creations of philosophy, function as road signs, indicating the direction of philosophical transcending. Thus there is no substitute for the profound discourse of the metaphysician, which speaks to us from the centuries; to assimilate it from its source in the history of philosophy is not only to know something that once was but to make it come to life.

The mass of sham philosophical knowledge taught in the schools originates in the hypostatization of entities that have served for a time as the signpost of philosophy but are always being transcended by it. Such hypostatized entities are nothing but the *capita mortua*, the ossuaries of the great metaphysical systems. To imagine that they confer knowledge is a philosophical perversion. In philosophizing we must not fall under the spell of the object that we use as a means of transcendence. We must remain masters of our thoughts and not be subjugated by them.

Yet in this intellectual transcendence, which is proper to philosophy and which is analogous to scientific forms, philosophy is less than science. For it does not gain any tangible results or any intellectually binding insight. There is no overlooking the simple fact that while scientific cognition is identical throughout the world, philosophy, despite its claim to universality, is not actually universal in any shape or form. This fact is the outward characteristic of the peculiar nature of philosophical truth. Although scientific truth is universally valid, it remains relative to method and assumptions; philosophical truth is absolute for him who conquers it in historical actuality, but its statements are not universally valid. Scientific truth is one and the same for all—philosophical truth wears multiple historical cloaks; each of these is the manifestation of a unique reality, each has its justification, but they are not identically transmissible.

The one philosophy is the *philosophia perennis* around which all philosophies revolve, which no one possesses, in which every genuine philosopher shares, and which nevertheless can never achieve the form of an intellectual edifice valid for all and exclusively true.

Thus philosophy is not only less but also more than science, namely, as the source of a truth that is inaccessible to scientifically binding knowledge. It is this philosophy that is meant in such definitions as: To philosophize is to learn how to die or to rise to godhead—or to know being qua being. The meaning of such definitions is: Philosophical thought is inward action; it appeals to freedom; it is a summons to transcendence. Or the same thing can be formulated differently: Philosophy is the act of becoming conscious of genuine being—or is the thinking of a faith in man that must be infinitely elucidated—or is the way of man's self-assertion through thinking.

But none of these propositions is properly speaking a definition. There is no definition of philosophy, because philosophy cannot be determined by something outside it. There is no genus above philosophy, under which it can be subsumed as a species. Philosophy defines itself, relates itself directly to godhead, and does not justify itself by any kind of utility. It grows out of the primal source in which man is given to himself.

To sum up: The sciences do not encompass all of the truth but only the exact knowledge that is binding to the intellect and universally valid. Truth has a greater scope, and part of it can reveal itself only to philosophical reason. Throughout the centuries since the early Middle Ages, philosophical works have been written under the title "On the Truth"; today the same task still remains urgent, i.e., to gain insight into the essence of truth in its full scope under the present conditions of scientific knowledge and historical experience.

The foregoing considerations also apply to the relation between science and philosophy. Only if the two are strictly distinguished can the inseparable connection between them remain pure and truthful.

Through research and study the university strives to achieve the great practical unity of the sciences and philosophy. At the university a philosophical view of the world has always been made manifest through scientific method.

The university is the meeting place of all sciences. In so far as these remain an aggregate, the university resembles an intellectual warehouse; but in so far as they strive toward unity of knowledge, it resembles a never-finished temple.

A century and a half ago this was still self-evident: the philosophical ideas that were assumed by the scientists in the various disciplines were brought to the highest light of consciousness by the philosophers. But the situation has changed. The sciences have become fragmented by specialization. It has come to be believed that scientific cognition, marked by the neatness of universally valid particular knowledge, could break away from philosophy.

Is the present dispersion of the sciences the ultimate and necessary stage? One might wish for a philosophy that would encompass and assimilate the whole tradition, that would be equal to the intellectual situation of our time, that would express the contents common to all of us, and this both in sublime intellectual constructions and in simple propositions capable of finding resonance in every man. Today we have no such philosophy.

Old university seals dating from the fifteenth century reveal figures wrought in gold which represent Christ distributing their tasks to the faculties. Even where such seals are still in use they no longer express the modern reality; yet they still bear witness to the task of unifying the whole.

Today neither theology nor philosophy creates a whole. Does the university still have a common spirit? As regards its organization, it still seems to constitute an ever-changing plan without symmetry or logic, never definitive, constantly in process of enlargement, a plan in which everything that achieves scientific status has its place. The most disparate elements meet. Not related by a knowledge of the whole, everyone is nevertheless compelled to see in this meeting something previously unknown, everyone learns to come into contact with highly unfamiliar things. Hence arises the intellectual life, the striving for greater expanse and freedom of thought. Thus a common spirit is no longer found in a faith binding to all but only in critical inquiry as such, in the recognition of the logically or empirically unascertainable, in the resolute refusal to perpetrate the *sacrificium intellectus*, in open-mindedness, in unlimited questioning, in integrity.

This spirit is the product of the last few centuries. Will the university content itself with this spirit forever? For philosophy this situation seems to offer extraordinary possibilities. But it would be absurd to draw up a programme for a task that can be carried out only by an intellectual world operating with a true sense of community, not by an individual.

So long as the philosopher retains his integrity, he is modestly aware of the limits of his knowledge. This must not be confused with another kind of modesty needed today, that of the *teacher* of philosophy. The best philosophers today are not perhaps to be found among those charged explicitly with the teaching of philosophy. For the philosophy *in* the sciences, which preserves us from dissipating our energies on things that are not worth knowing and which animates scientific inquiry, is the concrete philosophy that is embodied in the totality of a specific science. This philosophy thus becomes in a sense the spokesman for knowledge in general, provided that constant care is taken to see this particular domain in relation to all the knowable and thereby to anchor it in depth.

The teacher of philosophy in the service of such efforts is not a leader who lays down the law but an attentive and patient listener, eager to find meaning in the broadest interrelations.

The teacher of philosophy reveres the individual great philosophers, who are not specimens of a type but creators (such do not exist today), but he rejects the idolization of men, which began even in the academy of Plato, for even the greatest are men and err, and no one is an authority who must be obeyed by right.

And the teacher of philosophy has respect for each science whose insights are binding—but he condemns the scientific pride which imagines that everything can be known in its ultimate foundation or even goes so far as to suppose that it is known.

His ideal is that of a rational being coexisting with other rational beings. He wants to doubt, he thirsts for objections and attacks, he strives to become capable of playing his part in the dialogue of ever-deepening communication, which is the prerequisite of all truth and without which there is no truth.

His hope is that in the same measure as he becomes a rational being he may acquire the profound contents which can sustain man, that his will, in so far as his striving is honest, may become good through the direct help of the transcendent, without any human mediation.

As a teacher of philosophy, however, he feels that it is his duty not to let his students forget the great minds of the past, to preserve the various philosophical methods as an object of instruction, and to see to it that the sciences influence philosophical thinking; to elucidate the present age and at the same time to join his students in conquering a view of the eternal.

APPENDIX II

ON READING PHILOSOPHY

If it is true that philosophy concerns man as man, it must lie within our power to make it generally intelligible. It must be possible to communicate briefly certain fundamental ideas, though not of course the complex operations of systematic philosophy. It has been my intention to give an intimation of those elements in philosophy which are the concern of every man. But in so doing I have endeavoured not to disregard the essential, even where it seemed intrinsically difficult.

The present lectures are little more than sketches, covering but a small segment of the possibilities of philosophical thought. Many great ideas are not even touched upon. My aim has been to encourage my listeners to reflect on these matters for themselves.

For those who may seek guidance in their philosophical reflections I append what follows.

1. ON THE STUDY OF PHILOSOPHY

Philosophical thought is concerned with the ultimate, the authentic which becomes present in real life. Every man as man philosophizes.

But the developments of this thought cannot be understood at a glance. Systematic philosophy calls for study. Such study may be divided into three parts:

First: *Participation in scientific inquiry.* From its two

main roots in the natural sciences and in philology scientific discipline branches out into innumerable specialized fields. Experience in the sciences, their methods, their critical approach makes for the scientific attitude indispensable to honest philosophical endeavour.

Second: *The study of great philosophers*. We cannot find our way to philosophy without a knowledge of its history. In his journey upward the student draws nourishment from the great works. But he can succeed in his journey only through actual participation, through his own philosophical thinking which is awakened in study.

Third: *A conscientious approach to the conduct of daily life*, seriousness in crucial decisions, a sense of responsibility for our acts and experience.

To achieve a clear and true philosophy we must devote ourselves to all three aspects. Everyone, and particularly every young man, must decide exactly how he means to approach them; he can apprehend only the minutest fraction of their potentialities. These questions arise:

In which branch of science shall I seek specialized knowledge?

Which of the great philosophers shall I not only read but study intensively?

How shall I live?

Each man must answer these questions for himself. The answer must not be a fixed formula, it must not be definitive or external. The young in particular must preserve themselves in a state of potentiality and experiment.

I venture these maxims: proceed resolutely but do not run aground; test and correct, not haphazardly or arbitrarily but in a constructive spirit, retaining every experience as an effective force in your thinking.

2. ON PHILOSOPHICAL READING

When I read I wish first of all to understand what the author meant to say. But in order to understand what he meant I must understand not only his language but his subject matter as well. My understanding will depend on my knowledge of the subject.

It is through the understanding of texts that we set out to acquire our knowledge of the subject. Hence we must think of the subject itself and at the same time of what the author meant. One without the other makes the reading fruitless.

Since when I study a text I have the subject in mind, my understanding of the text undergoes an involuntary transformation. For a sound understanding both are necessary: immersion in the subject matter and return to a clear understanding of the author's meaning. In the first process I acquire philosophy, in the second historical insight.

Reading should be undertaken in an attitude compounded of confidence in the author and love for the subject he has taken up. At first I must read as though everything stated in the text were true. Only after I have allowed myself to be completely carried away, after I have been in the subject matter and then re-emerged as it were from its centre, can meaningful criticism begin.

How, in studying the history of philosophy, we make past philosophy our own may be elucidated on the basis of the three Kantian imperatives: think for yourself; in your thinking put yourself in the place of every other man; think in unanimity with yourself. These imperatives are endless tasks. Any anticipated solution making it appear that we have already fulfilled them is a delusion; we are always on our way to a solution. And in this history helps us.

Independent thinking does not spring from the void. What we think must have roots in reality. The authority of tradition awakens in us the sources anticipated in faith, by contact with them in the beginnings and in the historical fulfilments of philosophical thought. Any further study presupposes this confidence. Without it we should not take upon ourselves the trouble of studying Plato or Kant.

Our own philosophical thinking twines upward as it were round the historical figures. Through the understanding of their texts we ourselves become philosophers. But this confident learning is not obedience. In this following we test our own essence. This "obedience" is a trusting to guidance; we begin by accepting something as true; we do not break in immediately and constantly with critical reflections which paralyse what is our own true, though guided, movement. And this obedience is the respect which does not allow of easy criticism but only of a criticism which through our own conscientious effort comes closer and closer to the core of the matter until it is able to cope with it. The limit of obedience is that we recognize as true only what through our independent thinking has become our own conviction. No philosopher, not even the greatest, is in possession of the truth. *Amicus Plato, magis amica veritas.*

We arrive at the truth in independent thinking only if in our thinking we strive constantly *to put ourselves in the place of every other man.* We must learn to know what is possible for man. By seriously attempting to think what another has thought we broaden the potentialities of our own truth, even where we bar ourselves to the other's thinking. We learn to know it only if we venture to put ourselves entirely into it. The remote and alien, the extreme and the exception, even the anomalous all enjoin us to neglect no original thought, to miss no truth by blindness or indifference. Accordingly, the student of philosophy turns not only to the philosopher of his choice whom he studies without stint as his own; he turns also to the history of philosophy, in order to learn what was and what men have thought.

The study of history involves the danger of dispersion and noncommitment. The imperative *to think in unanimity with ourselves* is direct against the temptation to indulge too long in curiosity and the pleasure of contemplating diversity. What we learn from history should become a stimulus; it should either make us attentive or call us to question. The elements of history should not lie indifferently side by side in our minds. We ourselves must create friction between these elements which historical fact itself has not brought into exchange and contact. We must create a relation even among the most disparate elements.

All elements come together by being received into

the thinker's one self. To be unanimous with ourselves means to preserve our own thinking by relating
the separate, the contradictory, the diffuse, to a unity.
Universal history, intelligently assimilated, becomes a
unity, though an open one. The idea of the unity of the
history of philosophy, continuously shattered by
reality, is the driving principle in our learning.

3. WORKS ON THE HISTORY OF PHILOSOPHY

These works serve very diverse aims.

They may consist in collected texts, in simple des-
criptions of texts, biographies of the philosophers,
sociological accounts, investigations of influences and
stages of development. They may consist in descrip-
tions and discussions of the contents of works, in
analyses of their motivations, systems, methods.

There are works characterizing the mind or
principles of particular philosophers and whole epochs.
Finally, there are general works, culminating in the
histories of world philosophy.

The writer on the history of philosophy must be
equipped with philological insight, and he must also be
a philosopher capable of participating in the philosophical thought of the past. The truest historical conception will inevitably amount to original philosophy.

Hegel was the first philosopher who took a consciously philosophical view of the whole history of
philosophy. For this reason his history of philosophy
remains a magnificent achievement. But because of
its Hegelian principles it penetrates but also kills. All the
philosophers of the past live for a moment as in a won-
derfully illuminating spotlight; but then it suddenly

becomes apparent that Hegelian thinking cuts the heart out of them and buries their remains in the vast graveyard of history. Hegel was finished with the past because he believed he had encompassed the whole of it. His rational penetration is not candid exploration but destructive surgery, it is not enduring questioning but conquest and subjection, it is not a living-with but domination.

It is always advisable to read several accounts of history side by side in order to safeguard ourselves against accepting any one view as self-evident. If we read only one account its classifications force themselves upon us involuntarily.

It is also advisable to read no account without at least sampling the related original texts.

Finally, histories of philosophy may be used as reference works for literary orientation, and various philosophical lexicons are also useful.

4. TEXTS

For individual study it is worthwhile to acquire a limited library containing the really important texts. Any list upon which such a library might be based will be subject to personal modification. But there is a core which is almost universal, though even here the accent will vary; there is no universal accent that will be accepted by all.

It is a good idea to begin by specializing in one philosopher. It is of course desirable that this should be one of the great philosophers, but it is possible to find the way to philosophy through a philosopher of second or third rank. Any philosopher, thoroughly studied, leads step by step to philosophy and the history of philosophy as a whole.

For antiquity any bibliography is limited by the small number of extant texts, particularly of complete works, that have been preserved. For more recent centuries the texts are so abundant that, quite on the contrary, the difficulty lies in selecting one.

LIST OF NAMES. I

WESTERN PHILOSOPHY

ANCIENT PHILOSOPHY

Fragments of the Pre-Socratics (600–400).

Plato (428–348).

Aristotle (384–322).

Fragments of the Old Stoics (300–200). Seneca (d. A.D. 65), Epictetus (*ca.* A.D. 50–138), Marcus Aurelius (ruled A.D. 161–180).

Fragments of Epicurus (342–271). Lucretius (96–55).

The Sceptics. Sextus Empiricus (*ca.* A.D. 150), Cicero (106–43 B.C.), Plutarch (*ca.* A.D. 45–125).

Plotinus (A.D. 203–270).

Boethius (A.D. 480–525).

CHRISTIAN PHILOSOPHY

Church Fathers: St. Augustine (354–430).

Middle Ages: John Scotus Erigena (9th century). Anselm (1033–1109). Abelard (1079–1142). St. Thomas (1225–74). John Duns Scotus (d. 1308). Master Eckhart (1260–1327). William of Ockham (*ca.* 1300–50). Nicholas of Cusa (1401–64). Luther (1483–1546). Calvin (1509–64).

MODERN PHILOSOPHY

16th century: Machiavelli, Thomas More, Paracelsus, Montaigne, Bruno, Jacob Böhme, Bacon.

17th century: Descartes, Hobbes, Spinoza, Leibnitz, Pascal.

18th century:

ENGLISH RATIONALISTS: Locke, Hume.
FRENCH AND ENGLISH MORALISTS
   17th century: La Rochefoucauld, La Bruyère.
   18th century: Shaftesbury, Vauvenargues, Chamfort.
GERMAN PHILOSOPHY: Kant, Fichte, Hegel, Schelling.
19th century:
   GERMAN ACADEMIC PHILOSOPHY, e.g., The Younger Fichte,
   Lotze.
   THE ORIGINAL PHILOSOPHERS: Kierkegaard, Nietzsche.
Modern sciences as an area of philosophy:
   POLITICAL AND ECONOMIC PHILOSOPHY: Tocqueville, Lorenz
   von Stein, Marx.
   PHILOSOPHY OF HISTORY: Ranke, Burckhardt, Max Weber.
   NATURAL PHILOSOPHY: K. E. von Baer, Darwin.
   PSYCHOLOGICAL PHILOSOPHY: Fechner, Freud.

In roughly characterizing these men I shall venture a number of inadequate remarks. In no case do I expect to classify or dispose of any philosopher, although my statements will inevitably sound as if I did. I should like my remarks to be taken as questions. They are intended merely to call attention to certain things and perhaps to help some readers to find out where their own inclinations lead.

ON ANCIENT PHILOSOPHY

The Pre-Socratics have the unique magic that lies in the "beginnings." They are uncommonly difficult to understand correctly. We must attempt to disregard all the "philosophical education" which veils their immediacy in current habits of thought and speech. In the Pre-Socratics thought is working its way out of the original intuitive experience of being. In reading them we participate in man's first intellectual illuminations. The work of each of these great thinkers shows a unity and specificity of style that have never been equalled since. As only fragments have come down to us, the reader is tempted to read things into the text. The whole is still full of riddles.

Plato, Aristotle, Plotinus are the only ancient philosophers whose works have been preserved in any measure of completeness. These three occupy first place for the study of ancient philosophy.

Plato teaches the eternal, fundamental experiences of philosophy. The movement of his thought embraces the whole wealth of the Greek philosophy that had gone before. Amid the breakdown of his own age he stood at the frontier of every time. He perceived the world of the thinkable with the most independent openness. He achieved the clearest communication of his thoughts, but he communicated them in such a way that the mystery of philosophical endeavour becomes speech while remaining always present as mystery. In him all materiality is smelted down. The essential is the operation of transcending. Plato achieved the summit beyond which, it would seem, man cannot pass in his thinking. Down to the present day the strongest philosophical impulses have emanated from him. He has always been misunderstood, for he has no doctrine that can be learned and his teachings must always be acquired anew. In the study of Plato, as of Kant, we obtain no fixed knowledge but learn to philosophize for ourselves. All subsequent thinkers reveal themselves in their manner of understanding Plato.

From Aristotle we learn the categories which, since his time, have dominated Western thinking. He laid down the language (terminology) of philosophy, whether Aristotelian or anti-Aristotelian or conceived as transcending this entire plane of thinking.

Plotinus used the whole tradition of ancient philosophy as a means of expressing a wonderful metaphysic, original in mood, which has come down through the ages as *the* true metaphysic. Mystical serenity is communicated in the music of a speculation which remains unequalled and which re-echoes wherever men have thought metaphysically.

The Stoics, Epicureans, and Sceptics, the Platonists and Aristotelians (the later Academics and Peripatetics) created the universal philosophy of the educated classes of late antiquity for whom Cicero and Plutarch also wrote. Despite all the conflicting positions and constant polemics among them, they represent a world in common. Participation in all its aspects amounted to eclecticism, but it also characterizes the specifically limited fundamental attitude of these ancient centuries, the personal dignity, the continuity of a world in which the essentials were merely repeated, a world which was strangely finished and barren, yet in which men understood one another. This is the home of the cosmopolitan philosophy that still has currency today. Its last captivating figure is Boethius, whose *Consolatio philosophiae*, by virtue of its mood, beauty, and authenticity, is among the basic works of philosophy.

Since then, philosophical communities of education, concepts, style, and attitude have been realized by the clergy of the Middle Ages, the Humanists since the Renaissance, and in a weaker sense by the speculative, idealistic German philosophers between 1770 and

1850. The study of these societies is of great historical and sociological interest. It is important to understand the distance between the great philosophical creations and this universalizing form of thought. Humanism is particularly important because its peculiar source is not a great philosophy but an attitude toward tradition and learning, an attitude of openness and human freedom, without which our Western life would be impossible. Humanism (which merely became explicit in the Renaissance, in Pico, Erasmus, Marsilio Ficino, who can still be read profitably today) goes through every age, since the conscious *paideia* of the Greeks and since the cultivation of Greek influence in Rome in the age of the Scipios. In our day it has grown weak. Its disappearance would be a catastrophe of incalculable intellectual and human consequence.

ON CHRISTIAN PHILOSOPHY

Far the greatest of the Church Fathers is St. Augustine. The study of his works gives us the whole of Christian philosophy. Here we find innumerable, unforgettable formulations expressing that passionate, meditative inwardness that is lacking in ancient philosophy. His immeasurably rich work is full of repetitions, it is sometimes rhetorically diffuse, as a whole perhaps it is without beauty, yet in detail it gives terse and forceful expression to profound truths. We become familiar with his adversaries through the quotations and references in his polemics. Augustine's works remain to this day a spring from which all thinkers draw who seek to know the soul in its depths.

Scotus Erigena conceived an edifice of being, comprising God, nature and man, in Neoplatonic categories with dialectic freedom of development. He contributed a new mood of self-awareness and openness to the world. A man of learning, he knew Greek and translated Dionysius Areopagita. Working with traditional concepts, he erected a magnificent system, original in its attitude. He sought to define God as nature, and founded a new speculative mysticism which has enjoyed influence down to the present. His work is a product of ancient tradition, blended with deep Christian and philosophical faith.

The methodical thinking of the Middle Ages first becomes original with Anselm. Immediate metaphysical revelations are expressed in the dry language of logic and jurisprudence. While his logical argumentations and particularly his dogmatic propositions are alien to us, his ideas are still alive, in so far as we disregard their historical cloak of Christian dogmatism and take them in their universal human import as we do those of Parmenides.

Abelard teaches the energy of reflection, the roads of the logically possible, the method of dialectic contradiction as a means of exploring problems. By this extreme questioning through the confrontation of opposites he became the founder of the Scholastic method which achieved its summit in Thomas Aquinas; at the same time he sowed the seeds of disintegration in the naïve Christianity which had sustained men before him.

Thomas Aquinas erected the grandiose system which has been overwhelmingly accepted in the Catholic world down to our day, a system in which the kingdom of nature and the kingdom of grace, that which is accessible to reason and that which is accessible only to faith, the secular and the ecclesiastical, the confuted heretical positions and the element of truth in them, are encompassed in a unity which has been compared not without reason to the great cathedrals of the Middle Ages. He created a unity out of the products of medieval thought. In the light of his work the medieval philosophers were all precursors, down to Albert the Great with his organization of the material and his method of adapting Aristotle. Perhaps Thomas excels him only in his clarity and in the moderation and succinctness of his thinking. The mood and vision of this complete philosophical reality of the Middle Ages can be found in Dante's *Divine Comedy*.

Duns Scotus and William of Ockham broke through the structure of medieval thought at almost the very moment when it seemed to be complete. Still in a form that passed as orthodox, Duns Scotus spurs to thought by the profound difficulties which he found in the question of will and in the unique individuality of the Here and Now. Ockham exploded the Scholastic epistemology and laid the foundations of the modern theory of knowledge, with its endless horizons and its sense of human limitations. In the political sphere, as publicist for Louis the Bavarian, he shattered the claims of the church. Like all the medieval thinkers whose works have come down to us, he too was a believer in Christ (the unbelievers, sceptics, nihilists are known to us mostly through refutations and quotations). To this day there is no modern edition of

Ockham's works. They have not been translated into German. This is perhaps the only great gap still to be filled in the history of philosophy.

Nicholas of Cusa is the first philosopher of the Middle Ages whom we encounter in an atmosphere which seems to us our own. True, he remains entirely medieval in his faith, for in him the unity of ecclesiastical faith is still unbroken, the trust that the unity of the Catholic Church will one day embrace all nations. But in his philosophy he no longer projects one system; like Thomas, he does not make use of the Scholastic method, which logically apprehends all tradition in its contradictions, but turns directly to the matter in hand, whether it be metaphysical (transcendant) or empirical (immanent). Thus he employs special methods based on his own intuitions, and finds a wonderful divine being, which in these speculations is revealed in a new way. In this being of the godhead he sees the realities of the world, and in such a way that speculation opens the path to empirical and mathematical insights which become the instruments of the intuition of God. His is an all-embracing thought, lovingly close to reality and yet transcending it. The world is not circumvented but itself shines in the light of transcendence. This is a metaphysic which is still indispensable. The time spent in exploring it may be counted among the happy hours of the philosopher.

With Luther it is different. To study him is indispensable. He is a theological thinker who despises philosophy, speaks of the whore reason, yet he himself thought out the basic existential ideas without which present philosophy would scarcely be possible. The combination of passionate seriousness of faith and of opportunistic shrewdness, of depth and hatred, of brilliant penetration and coarse bluster makes it a duty, almost a torment to study him. This man gives forth a profoundly antiphilosophical atmosphere.

Calvin's greatness lies in disciplined, methodic form, iron logic, unswerving and dauntless adherence to principles. But his loveless intolerance makes him, in his theoretical as in his practical activities, the repellent antithesis of philosophy. It is good to have looked him in the face in order to recognize this spirit wherever, in veiled or fragmentary form, it is manifested in the world. He is the supreme incarnation of that Christian intolerance against which there is no weapon but intolerance.

ON MODERN PHILOSOPHY

In contrast to ancient and medieval philosophy, modern philosophy forms no comprehensive whole but is an agglomeration of the most disparate, unrelated efforts, full of fine systematic structures, none of which is actually dominant. It is extraordinarily rich, full of the concrete and of bold, free abstractions, in constant relation to new science. Its works are differentiated along national lines, written in Italian, German, French, and English, in addition to those carry-overs from the Middle Ages that were still composed in Latin.

We shall attempt a characterization of modern philosophy in chronological order.

The sixteenth century is rich in heterogeneous, extraordinary personal creations, which move us by their immediacy. They remain rich sources.

In the political sphere Machiavelli and More initiated the modern approach to history as a chain of causes and effects. Despite their outmoded trappings their works are still graphic and interesting.

Paracelsus and Böhme show us that world, equally rich in profundity and superstition, with clarity and in uncritical confusion, which today is known as theosophy, anthroposophy, cosmosophy. Rich in intuitions and images, they lead into a maze. We must discern the rational structure that lies hidden in the cabbalistic quaintness and, particularly with Böhme, in dialectical subtleties.

Montaigne is the type of man grown independent, without desire for realization in the world. His morality and opinions, integrity and shrewdness, sceptical openness and sense of the practical are expressed in modern form. The reading of Montaigne is immediately captivating, philosophically it is a perfect expression for this form of life, but at the same time it is in a sense paralysing. His earthbound self-sufficiency is a delusion.

Bruno in contrast is the infinitely struggling philosopher, consuming himself in inadequacy. He has knowledge of the limits and believes in the supreme. His dialogue on the *eroici furori* is a basic work of the philosophy of enthusiasm.

Bacon is known as the founder of modern empiricism and of the modern sciences. Both erroneously. For he did not understand true modern science, the mathematical science of nature, then at its beginnings, and this science would never have come into being by his methods. But in an enthusiasm for the new, characteristic of the Renaissance, Bacon ardently espoused the ideas that knowledge is power, that vast technical possibilities lay ahead, that illusions must be replaced by a rational approach to reality.

The seventeenth century brings the philosophy of rational construction, of great systems erected by neat logical development. The air seems to have cleared, but the rich images and intuitions have silently vanished. Modern science is at hand, assuming the character of a pattern for all thought.

Descartes is the founder of this new philosophical world, and beside him Hobbes. Descartes' perverted conception of science and philosophy made his influence disastrous. Because of this, and because of the basic fallacy that is obvious in his work, we should study him today in order to know the road that is to be avoided. Though Hobbes developed a system of being, his greatness lies in his political theory, revealing with impressive logic elements of reality that with him enter the human consciousness for all time.

Spinoza is the metaphysician who with traditional and Cartesian concepts expresses a philosophical faith; he is original in the metaphysical mood which he alone possessed among the philosophers of his time. Of the philosophers of his century he alone has followers today.

Pascal represents a reaction to the absolutization of science and the system. His thinking dominates both, it has the same precision but greater integrity and depth.

Leibnitz, as universal as Aristotle, richer than all the philosophers of this century in ideas and inventions, always creative, always intelligent, is in his metaphysics without the greatness that comes of a basic attitude which is profoundly human.

The eighteenth century shows for the first time a broader stream of philosophical literature addressed to a general public. It is the century of the Enlightenment.

The English Enlightenment has its first representative figure in Locke. He provided the English society growing out of the revolution of 1688 with its intellectual and political groundwork. Hume is the brilliant analyst; an intelligent writer, even when tedious, he does not strike us as commonplace. His scepticism is the bold, unflinching integrity of a man who dares to stand at the limits and face the unfathomable, without speaking of it.

Both in France and in England there was a literature of aphorisms and essays by observers of men and society, whom we call "moralists." They strove to bring a philosophical attitude into psychology. In the seventeenth century the work of La Rochefoucauld and La Bruyère, in the eighteenth century that of Vauvenargues and Chamfort, grew out of the world of the court. Shaftesbury was the philosopher of an aesthetic discipline of life.

Along with a systematic energy and an openness to what is deepest and what is most remote, the great German philosophers have an intellectual vigour and wealth of ideas that make them an indispensable foundation for all serious philosophical thought: Kant, Fichte, Hegel, Schelling.

Kant: for us the decisive step toward awareness of being; precision in the intellectual operation of transcending; an ethos growing out of our inadequacy;

vastness of conception and humanitarian feeling; like Lessing, a personification of radiant reason. A noble man.

Fichte: speculation carried to the point of fanaticism, frantic attempts at the impossible, brilliant construction, moral eloquence. He initiated a destructive trend of extremism and intolerance.

Hegel: mastery and many-sided elaboration of the dialectic categories; explored the full range of intellectual attitudes, effected the most comprehensive summation of Western history.

Schelling: indefatigable ponderings on the ultimate, broached disquieting mysteries; failed as creator of a system; opened up new paths.

The nineteenth century represents transition, dissolution and consciousness of dissolution, expansion of the material world, scientific scope. The philosophical impetus dwindled in philosophers turned professor, producing pale, arbitrary, unconvincing systems and studies on the history of philosophy which for the first time made the whole historical material accessible. The authentic philosophical drive survived in exceptions, scarcely recognized by their contemporaries, and in science.

German academic philosophy is instructive, full of conscientiousness and zeal; however, it no longer draws from the essence of man but derives from the bourgeois world with its cultural ideals, its well-meaning seriousness, and its limitations. Even its more important figures, such as the younger Fichte and Lotze, will be studied for their edification, not for their substance.

The original philosophers of this era are Kierkegaard and Nietzsche. Both without system, both exceptions and victims. They are aware of the catastrophe, utter astounding truths, and show no way out. In them the age is documented by the most merciless self-criticism in human history.

Kierkegaard: forms of spiritual action, profound intellectual commitment. In him everything, particularly congealed Hegelian thought, is made fluid again. Violently Christian.

Nietzsche: endless reflection, auscultation and questioning of all things; digs deeply but discovers no foundations, except for new paradoxes. Violently anti-Christian.

The modern sciences become vehicles of a philosophical attitude, not in their general concerns but in numerous though separate personalities. Here are a few names only as examples.

Political and social philosophy: Tocqueville apprehended the course of the modern world toward democracy, through sociological knowledge of the *ancien régime*, of the French Revolution, and of the United States of America. His preoccupation with freedom, his sense of human dignity and of authority, led him to inquire realistically into the inevitable and the possible. He was a man and scientist of the first order. On the basis of the political actions and ideas of the French since 1789, Lorenz von Stein interpreted the events of the first half of the nineteenth century in terms of the polarity between state and society. He considered the question of Europe's destiny. Marx utilized these insights, developed them in economic constructions, infused them with hatred against existing forms, and endowed them with chiliastic aims for the future. In the underprivileged and hopeless proletarians of all nations a light of hope shall be born which will unite them and make them into a power capable of overturning the economic, sociological, and political status quo to create a world of justice and freedom.

Philosophy of history: In an atmosphere of Goethe and Hegel, Ranke developed a critical approach to history in the service of a universalistic view which is itself a philosophy even though it appears to reject philosophy. Jacob Burckhardt looked upon himself as a kind of priest of historical education, revealed the greatness and the blessings of historical memory, looked on salvation and doom with a fundamental pessimistic sense of standing at the end of a world whose glory exists only in such memory. Max Weber relaxed all prejudices, inquired by every means into the reality of history, clarified contexts in such a way that most earlier historiography seems pale, inadequate, and vague. Theoretically and practically he demonstrated the conflict between values and knowledge; he opened up new paths by humbly testing our knowledge of reality and rejecting all approximations and rash generalizations.

Natural philosophy: K. E. von Baer, by way of exploratory research, created a magnificent vision of the organic world in its fundamental characters. Darwin, his diametrical opposite, reduced this vision to a system of causalities, which implies the destruction of any sense of authentic life.

Psychological philosophy: Fechner established a methodical, experimental study of the relation between the psychological and physical factors in sense perception (psychophysics); this he conceived as part of a logical but actually fantastic theory of the animation of all life and all things. In his debunking psychology Freud naturalized and trivialized the sublime insights of Kierkegaard and Nietzsche. A barren, hateful weltanschauung masked by humanitarian forms was indeed appropriate to an age whose hypocrisy it pitilessly dissected, but Freud failed to see that this world was not the whole world.

LIST OF NAMES. II

CHINA AND INDIA

Chinese Philosophy

Lao Tse (6th century B.C.); Confucius (6th century B.C.); Mo Tse (second half of the 5th century B.C.); Chuang Tse (4th century B.C.).

Indian Philosophy

Upanishads (roughly 1000–400 B.C.); Pali Canon of Buddhism; texts from the Mahabharata (1st century B.C.). Bhagavad-Gita, etc.; Kautilya's Arthashastra; Shankara (9th century A.D.).

As thus far accessible to us in translations and interpretations, Chinese and Indian philosophy seem far inferior to Western philosophy in scope, in development, and in inspiring formulations. For us Western philosophy remains the main object of study. It is indeed an exaggeration to say that all we understand of Asiatic philosophy is what we would understand without it through our own philosophy. But it is true that most interpretations lean so heavily on theWestern categories that even for those who do not understand the oriental languages the error is perceptible.

Hence, though the parallel between the three developments—China, India, the West—is historically sound, it gives us a distorted picture in that it seems to place equal emphasis on all three. For us this is not the case. Despite those indispensable insights which we owe to Asiatic thinking, the main ideas which animate us are those of Western philosophy. Only in Western philosophy do we find the clear distinctions, the precise formulations of problems, the scientific orientation, the thorough discussions, the sustained thought, which to us are indispensable.

LIST OF NAMES. III

PHILOSOPHY IN RELIGION, LITERATURE, AND ART

Religion: The Bible; the texts collected in source books of religious history.

Literature: Homer; Aeschylus, Sophocles, Euripides; Dante; Shakespeare, Goethe, Dostoyevsky.

Art: Leonardo, Michelangelo, Rembrandt.

In order to possess ourselves of the contents of philosophy down through its history we must read and reread the philosophers in the restricted sense; we must obtain a clear view of the development of the sciences; and we must allow ourselves to be moved by the great works of religion, literature, and art. We should not keep turning to new and varied works but immerse ourselves in those which are truly great.

The Great Works

Some few works of philosophy are in their own way as infinite as great works of art. They contain more thought than the author himself knew. True, every profound idea implies consequences of which the thinker is not immediately aware. But in the great philosophies it is the totality itself which conceals the infinite. An astonishing harmony pervades the very contradictions, so that even they become an expression of truth. The complexity of thought, while achieving clarity in the foreground, reveals unfathomable depths. The more patiently we study these works the more wonderful they seem to us. Such are the works of Plato, of Kant, Hegel's *Phenomenology of Mind*—but each for reasons of its own. In Plato we find balanced form, supreme lucidity, the keenest knowledge of method, artistic expression of philosophical truth, without sacrifice of clarity and force. In Kant we have the greatest integrity, scupulous weighing of every word, the most sublime clarity. Hegel is less scrupulous, occasionally carried away by his own facility; but these defects are counterbalanced by wealth of ideas, creative genius, which reveals deep meanings though it does not integrate them in his own philosophy, which is full of violence and deception, shows a tendency toward dogmatic scholasticism and aestheticism.

Philosophies vary exceedingly in rank and in kind. It is a question of philosophical destiny whether or not in my youth I entrust myself to the study of a great philosopher and to which of the great philosophers I entrust myself.

We may say that everything can be found in one of the great works. Through a great work we make our way upward through the whole realm of philosophy. By thorough study of one sublime lifework I find a centre, from which and toward which everything else may be illuminated. Everything else is drawn into the study of this work. In connection with it we gain an orientation in the whole history of philosophy, learn at least to find our way about it, gain impressions through samplings of original tests, gain an intimation of its other works. The thorough study of one philosopher prevents us from overestimating our knowledge of the doctrines we have studied less thoroughly.

A young man might welcome advice as to which philosopher he should select. But everyone must make this choice for himself. All we can do is to bring certain things to his notice. This choice is a fundamental decision. Perhaps it will follow from groping attempts. It may take years to form. Nevertheless some advice can be given. An old counsel is to study Plato and Kant since they cover all the essentials. In this I concur.

It is not a choice to let yourself be carried away by fascinating reading, as for example by Schopenhauer or Nietzsche. Choice means study with all the means at your disposal. It means a growing into the whole history of philosophy from the standpoint of one of its great manifestations. A work which does not lead along this road is an unfortunate choice, although ultimately every philosophical work, when really studied, must be in some way rewarding.

To choose a great philosopher for the study of his works does not mean to limit yourself to him. On the contrary, when you study one great philosopher, you should also consider another who is very different from him. If you restrict yourself to one, even the most unprejudiced philosopher, the result will be bias. Philosophy is incompatible with any deification of man, in which one man is regarded as an exclusive master. And the very essence of philosophical thought is openness to the truth as a whole, not to barren, abstract truth but to truth in the diversity of its supreme realizations.

BIBLIOGRAPHY

THOSE READERS WHO wish to look more closely into my philosophical writings may consult the following brief bibliography.

My two principal philosophical works are
1. *Philosophie.* 2 ed., Heidelberg-Berlin, Springer-Verlag, 1948.
2. *Von der Wahrheit.* Munich, R. Piper, 1948.

Short works treating the subject matter of these radio talks in greater detail:
1. *Der philosophische Glaube.* Munich, R. Piper, 1948; Zürich, Artemis-Verlag, 1948. English ed.: *The Perennial Scope of Philosophy*, trans. by Ralph Manheim. New York, Philosophical Library, 1949; London, Routledge and Kegan Paul, 1950.
2. *Vernunft und Existenz.* 2 ed., Bremen, Storm-Verlag, 1947.
3. *Philosophie und Wissenschaft.* Zürich, Artemis-Verlag, 1948.

On contemporary philosophy:
1. *Die geistige Situation der Zeit.* 7 ed., Berlin, W. de Gruyter, 1949. English ed.:

Man in the Modern Age. London, Routledge and Kegan Paul, 1934.

2. *Vom Ursprung und Ziel der Geschichte.* Zürich, Artemis-Verlag, 1949; Munich, R. Piper, 1949. English ed.: *The Origin and Goal of History*, London, Routledge and Kegan Paul (in preparation).

3. *Vom Europaischen Geist.* Munich, R. Piper, 1947. English ed.: *The European Spirit*, London, S.C.M. Press, 1948.

Works devoted to individual philosophers:

1. *Descartes und die Philosophie.* 2 ed., Berlin, W. de Gruyter, 1947.

2. *Nietzsche.* 3 ed., Berlin, W. de Gruyter, 1949.
   Nietzsche und das Christentum. Hameln, Bücherstube Seifert, 1946.

3. *Max Weber.* 2 ed., Bremen, Storm-Verlag, 1947.

On philosophy as manifested in the concrete sciences:

1. *Allgemeine Psychopathologie.* 5 ed., Heidelberg-Berlin, Springer-Verlag, 1947.

2. *Strindberg und van Gogh.* 3 ed., Bremen, Storm-Verlag, 1949.

Articles in English:

"Rededication of German Scholarship," trans. by M. Zuckerlandl, *American Scholar*, 15 (April, 1946), No. 2, 180-188.

"Is Europe's Culture Finished?" trans. by E. Basch, *Commentary*, 4 (December, 1947), 518-526.

"Axial Age of Human History," trans. by R. Manheim, *Commentary*, 6 (November, 1948), 430-435.

"Goethe and Our Future," *World Review* (London), June-July, 1949.

"Zu Nietzsches Bedeutung in der Geschichte der Philosophie," trans. by Ralph Manheim, to be published in *Partisan Review* under the tentative title "Nietzsche's Significance for the History of Philosophy."

This book originated in twelve radio lectures commissioned by the Basel radio station.

INDEX

INDEX

Communication: of truth, 13, 25–7; mysticism not communicable, 35; universal human readiness for, 91; and unity of mankind, 106–8; in the philosophical life, 122 *et seq.*

Communications before Christian era, 135

Community, security in, 21

Comprehensive, the, 13, 28–38; reached through certainty of existence, 43; and philosophical faith, 94; awareness of, 125

Comprehensive consciousness of God, 46–7

Conditional imperatives, 55

Conduct, aims and, 54–5

Confucius (551–478 B.C.), 99, 133, 190

Consciousness, 33, 36

Contemplation: pure, of mystics, 80–1; religious and philosophic, 122 *et seq.*

Cosmological proof of existence of God, 42–3

Cosmologies, "scientific", 76

Creation, free, source of philosophical thought, 9

Creative originality, 11

Cultures, growth of, 97

Dante, Alighieri (1265–1321), 181, 191

Darwin, Charles (1809–82), 176, 189

Dasein (=being-there), oriented toward environment, 32

Death, 20; and witness, 53

Death urge, 53

Decision, existential, demanded by unconditional imperative, 56

Deification of man, 45

Descartes, René (1596–1650), 18–19, 24, 134, 153, 175, 185

Despair, 20

Despotic Empires, rise of, 102

Determinacy, implications of, 30

Deutero-Isaiah, 100

Development and progress in philosophy, 140–1

Devil, serving the, 83

Devotion, unlimited, to God, the authentic mode of existence, 83–4

Dialectical method of Marx and Hegel, 154–6

Dichotomy: subject-object, 29 *et seq.*; meaning of, 30–1; two-fold, 30–1; implications of, 31; three modes of, 31–3; result of awareness of, 37–8

Differentiation, levels of, between good and evil, 59–62

Dignity of man, 91

Discussion, demanded by statement, 86–7

Disintegration, visible signs of present, 25

Doctrine of categories as structures, 78

Dogmatism of independence, 111

Doubt, a source of philosophy, 18–19, 24

Duns Scotus, John (1265–1308), 175, 181–2

Eckhart, Master (1260–1327), 175

Egypt, civilization of, 98

Elijah the prophet, 100

Enlightenment: faith and, 85–95; lack of faith and the, 87; demands of, 87; definition of, 88; ambivalence of, 88–90; attacks on, 89–90; nature of, 89

Enthusiasm, 184

Environment, *Dasein* (being-there) oriented toward, 32

Epictetus (A.D. 50–138), 175; on source of philosophy, 19

Epicureans, 178

Epicurus (342–271 B.C.), 175

Erasmus, Desiderius (1466–1536), 179

Eternal, to partake in the, 56

Ethical level of differentiation between good and evil, 59–60, 61–2

Euripides (484–407 B.C.), 191

European philosophy, modern, 136

Evil: definition of, 59; true, 59–60; antithesis of good and, 59–62

Existence: wonder of, 10; oriented toward God, 32–3; and freedom, 45; empirical, and the unconditional imperative, 52

Existentialism, 20*n*.

Failure, reality of, 22–3

Faith, 22; rooted in the Comprehensive, 36; nature of, 51; and

Simon.

INDEX